HOLIDAYS WITH KIDS

HOLIDAYS WITH KIDS

PAMELA HYDE   CAROLINE POOK   SUSAN YORK

PIATKUS

© 1987 Pamela Hyde, Caroline Pook, Susan York

First published in 1987 by Judy Piatkus (Publishers) Limited
5 Windmill Street, London W1P 1HS

British Library Cataloguing in Publication Data

Hyde, Pamela
  Holidays with kids.
  1. Vacations 2. Family recreation
  I. Title   II. Pook, Caroline III. York, Susan
  910.2'02   GV182.8

  ISBN 0–86188–587–2
  ISBN 0–86188–577–5 PbK

Designed by Paul Saunders
Cartoons by Ruth Boothby
Cover illustrated by Rowan Clifford

Typeset in 10/12pt VIP Plantin by
D. P. Media Limited, Hitchin, Herts
Printed and bound by
Mackays of Chatham Ltd

Contents

Preface

We do not claim to be travel experts, or even experts on child care, but just three mothers who were concerned when we heard for the umpteenth time from our friends about disappointing holidays. We were motivated to produce a booklet to raise funds for the Clapham Branch of the National Childbirth Trust and the response to this was so enthusiastic that the material has been expanded and updated to produce this book. We have tried to cover every aspect of choosing, planning and preparing for a holiday for families with children under 16.

We have drawn on our own experiences and those of parents all over Britain plus information gained from many other sources. We are particularly grateful to the many people who sent us details of their experiences or who let us grill them about recent holidays. We were amazed how much information appears in the media each year, but how little of it is coordinated in a useful way. We have prepared the book as a consumer guide and have included information direct from hundreds of brochures. Some of the information in this book will date quickly and, although we have made every effort to check it, we cannot claim that it is all entirely correct.

We plan to update and revise the book and would be very pleased to receive your comments and details of your holiday experiences.

We are indebted to our children: Edward, Joanna, Helen, Robert, Eleanor and last, but not least, William, who have so far taken 26 holidays plus numerous weekend trips and visits to relatives. We are also grateful for the support of David, Chris, and Richard and the many friends and relatives who took the children off our hands whilst we did our research. And, finally, thanks go to Tony and Will for the use of their word processors.

How to Use this Book

General Information on the various types of holiday discussed in the book is included in the section on HOLIDAYS IN THE BRITISH ISLES. Naturally, much of the same advice applies to holidays abroad, so we advise you to read the general remarks in that section first, no matter where you eventually decide to go.

Addresses of all the companies, organisations and publications mentioned are included in the appendix, together with the full names. The book list gives prices and publishers of all the books mentioned.

The term half-board is used where breakfast and one other meal is provided; full-board means that all meals are included.

The relative costs of various types of holidays are suggested broadly in the price guidelines. British holidays and Activity holidays, unless otherwise stated, are quoted in terms of one week on a half-board basis (if applicable) excluding travel. Foreign holidays are quoted in terms of two weeks on a half-board basis (again where applicable) including travel or an element of travel. We have assumed the average family to be two adults and two fare-paying children, although the section on single parent holidays does, of course, assume only one adult. The guideline prices always relate to high season, which we define as English School Summer Holidays (i.e. 20th July to 31st August) unless otherwise stated, and are taken from the Summer 1986 or Winter 1986/7 programmes.

The discounts shown in the tables apply to the Summer 1986 and Winter 1986/7 programmes. The discounts and free offers for 1987 were not available at the time of writing and operators were unwilling to tell us their future plans, either because they had not been finalised or because it was a closely guarded secret.

Ages Where age ranges are shown relating to discounts and child prices, these apply to the age of the child on the date of outward travel, or the date of arrival if a non-inclusive holiday. It does not apply to the age on the date of booking.

Elsewhere **children's ages** are cited as guidelines; naturally, you are the best judge of your own child's physical ability and mental development.

Introduction

Where are you and the children going for your holiday this year? Will it be a success, a disaster or just another holiday? We were prompted to write this book after hearing about so many disappointing holidays, the culmination of a whole year's saving and months of anticipation.

Holidays are the benchmarks by which we measure our children's development and achievements: 'He must have been able to walk by the time he was 14 months as he was really confident during that week on the Isle of Wight' . . . We can all remember our own childhood holidays, but not the routine events in between. We reinforce this by taking most of our photographs whilst away, so we can ill afford to make these times significant by disasters. Be prepared for children not to remember the events you expect. The funfair in Provence has stayed in the memory of the youngsters of one family, but the wonderful Roman remains have faded completely.

This book aims to help you avoid the pitfalls and to ensure that good planning and preparation give you the best chance of a successful holiday. However, as it is mainly based on personal experiences, we cannot give you the ultimate statement on what is good or bad. A memorable holiday for one family can be tedious and boring for another. Nevertheless, there do seem to be certain experiences in common and where we have received specific comments or several reports with similar reactions we have included them. It is worth saying, however, that where we were told of particularly miserable holidays, those involved usually blamed themselves or the weather.

Although this book includes a chapter on children going on holiday by themselves, it is principally about family holidays. Holidaying together is an experience you can all enjoy and learn from; the children will gain confidence and have a better understanding of life. Your children will save you from the worst excesses of sightseeing and their social antics will give you unusual and unexpected encounters with other people, and you may be led into all sorts of activities which you would not normally consider. In a life interspersed with dancing lessons, football training and Brownies, a holiday is one of the few periods of the year when you all sit down to eat together.

Whatever sort of holiday you choose it is likely that you will still be on duty 24 hours a day. You know only too well what your small child might do in those few moments when you rush off to fetch a jumper or turn round to pay for a ticket.

What Sort of Holiday?

Only you know whether you are longing for a sunny beach, long healthy walks or plenty of action. But before you decide from the ideas in this book, you might like to consider some of the points made in this section.

Time to yourself

Even the most doting of parents with children usually want a little time to themselves when on holiday, so select a holiday with something to occupy the children, whether it be new friends or organised activities. If you want the latter there are many holidays to choose from which include schemes to occupy every age group, from 0 to 16, for at least part of the day. If you don't relish the structured type of holiday which might be accompanied by an organised playscheme, perhaps granny would come with you, or you could share your holiday with friends.

Chores

Do you really want to take the kitchen sink with you as well? If you are renting self-catering accommodation, try not simply to exchange slaving over one hot stove for another. Try to arrange for someone else to clean up, particularly on the last day, and budget for some takeaways and some meals out if you can. Also remind your spouse and older children that help will be required on an *equal* basis.

Conflicting interests

Spend time reflecting on the needs of everyone going on the holiday. It can be difficult if, say, your 8 year old is not interested in the activities of the 3 year old. Parents can take it in turns to look after different children and excursions can be split between the interests of various members of the family, including the parents.

If you are not going on a special interest or activity holiday, think about what you are all going to do each day, and in the evenings too. Are your older children ready for a bit of disco visiting on their own? *You* may need to unwind but children do not, so you will have to compromise.

Older children will want plenty of activity, so beach-centred holidays should offer more than rock pools: good swimming, sports facilities, boats and so forth will occupy them some of the time. Similarly, an inland or mountain holiday should aim to provide more than scenic beauty – cycling or riding for instance.

The bucket and spade formula takes a lot of beating for children from 1 to 8 but they will also like other diversions such as a swimming pool or playground. Babies at the crawling and sand-eating stage will probably not be happy on a beach for long. Much later on, you will find the beach comes back into fashion, when 'late-nite' barbecues, 'coketails' and daytime preening afford an opportunity to ogle the opposite sex. Most importantly, children over 2 need other children to play or socialise with, otherwise you will end up organising them the whole time, just as you would at home.

Making friends

If you want to meet other people on holiday then you need to be wary of the language barrier, although getting over the hurdle is sometimes the way to amusing incidents. You might find your family rather isolated in a hotel, camping site or club where another nationality predominates and all entertainment and social activity is offered in another language. If it worries you, choose a resort which is popular with English language speakers.

Choosing Where to Go

The first choice most people make is whether to go abroad or to stay in Britain. It is commonly felt that the familiarity of Britain makes a holiday much simpler with children as there will be no problems of language, strange food, odd smells and unfamiliar customs. Although all this is true, it is balanced by the more easy-going attitudes to children, more relaxed licensing laws and more welcoming restaurants in many countries, and the milder climate in southern Europe where the holiday is less likely to be spoilt by the weather.

The second major decision may be the distance you are prepared to travel.

Does the disruption of moving between two centres outweigh the possible benefits? The children will take time to settle again, you will have to clear up and pack twice, etc.

Once you have selected your destination (or alternative destinations) obtain as much information about it as you can from some of the following sources:

A wide range of travel brochures, as they each cover the same areas in different ways.

Travel books and guidebooks borrowed from the library or friends, or bought from larger branches of W H Smith or a bookshop. If you find map-reading easy, a large-scale map will tell you a lot about walks, beaches and the size of towns and villages. Ordnance Survey maps of Britain can be acquired from the library, while for all other commonly visited countries you are sure to be able to get what you want from Edward Stanford Ltd, 12 Long Acre, London WC2 (01-836 1321).

Leaflets and other free literature from the appropriate tourist offices. This may include lists of accommodation, for which you sometimes have to pay.

A chat with friends who have been there in the past.

Guides to the coast and beaches and, more specifically, *The Golden List*, £2 plus SAE, from the Coastal Anti-pollution League, which identifies the good and bad among the beaches of England and Wales. You could also look at the *Illustrated Guide to Britain's Coast*.

Ask your travel agent Although wonderful places for collecting brochures, they are not always as good as they might be at giving information on what is available. Once you have visited several you may conclude that the independent outlets are more informative than the chains.

The Travel Agents' Gazetteer held by the agents, which gives excellent, and fairly candid, descriptions of resorts in many countries, although it excludes France and northern Europe. It also contains details on lots of hotels, with maps showing their exact location and whether the beach is sand or shingle. One travel agent described the gazetteer to us as the 'Put-you-off book' as so many hotels and resorts fared badly. This is no reason for you not to try and persuade him to lend you last year's copy!

Hogg Robinson *Fact Files* which are on display in all this travel agent's branches. They cover all the holidays that they sell, and as well as candid reports on hotels and resorts they contain good safety tips country by country.

Choosing When to Go

Although, under the 1944 Education Act, children are allowed to be absent from school for up to two weeks a year, many parents are reluctant to take their children out of school for two consecutive weeks at any time other than at the end of the summer term, when the emphasis shifts from lessons to outdoor activities. Most parents are particularly unwilling for their children to miss school in September when, although a good time to go on holiday weather-wise, new teachers are encountered and new friendships cemented.

Most of us take our annual fortnight's break during the summer school holidays when prices are at their highest and resorts most crowded. Those with unusual term dates should capitalise on their advantage and travel while most children are still in school. If your child has a critical birthday in the holiday season which puts the price of the holiday up, then try to travel before that date.

But what is the alternative for parents with school age children who do not want them to miss a fortnight from school?

You can take advantage of half-terms (perhaps added to one week off school) when prices are lower but weather less reliable. Or you could limit yourself to one week away. The Mediterranean at Easter is very pleasant, although the sea is only warm enough for the hardy. Little ones will have relatively empty beaches to play on, while older children who play tennis or ride will find the climate perfect and booking unnecessary. For hot weather you need to go further south to Morocco or the Canaries where you will pay high season prices and meet high season crowds.

You will see many brochures advertising foreign holidays in the 'Winter Sun' and offering bargains in tantalising places. We have had reports of winter holidays ranging from tremendous success stories to downright disasters. Parents told us of wonderful, cheap, holidays sight-seeing and exploring in spring sunshine, seeing the Algarve, Majorca and the Italian Riviera as the locals see them. The few who described unmitigated disasters attributed them to poor weather, lack of other children to play with or 'nothing to do all day'. Undoubtedly you will find closed shops and restaurants, restricted public transport, and hotels more than half empty. If you want a lively holiday in winter you would be better off considering skiing or paying more and going further afield.

If you are attracted by the idea of going abroad out of season you should look for a hotel or apartment complex with an indoor pool or a mini-club as these tend to attract families with children. The pool provides a focus for activity in those awkward hours between 5 pm and 7 pm when it is cool outside and adults tend to gravitate towards the bar.

For those with under 5s we can only stress 'go in term-time while you can' – a piece of advice passed to us time and time again. The sun is less likely to burn sensitive skins and the prices less likely to burn holes in pockets. Resorts are less crowded, although beaches may look a bit like playgroup outings.

Who to Go With

For some families, particularly those going on a self-catering holiday with no built-in amusements, the success or otherwise of the holiday depends on sharing it with others. For the children success means someone to play with, while for adults it means someone to share the chores with, the pleasure of other adult company and the chance to be free of their own child for an hour or two each day.

Sharing with another family

Children over 2 years usually need the company of others of similar age. Therefore, if you do not have a great brood of your own who play happily with one another you may consider sharing your holiday with another family. This is most likely to work out well if the children already get on with one another . . . do not expect them to like each other just because their parents are friends! It is important that their ages and temperaments are compatible: a 1 year old can be a real bore to an 18 month old (let alone to everyone else).

Either go with someone you know extremely well (with whom you have at least spent weekends together as families), or with someone you do not know but with whom you might have something in common. Do not share a holiday if it could harm the friendship: one mother told us 'we had to strike my best school friend off our Christmas card list after that holiday.'

Sharing a holiday does not necessarily mean communal living. You can choose separate villas, apartments or tents in the same complex. This arrangement allows you to have some family life of your own as other people's children can be irritating after a while. Also, if you share accommodation the children may keep each other awake. Children establish their own pecking order, and whether your child is aggressive or timid, tensions can develop between parents as well as between children when there is bullying or quarrelling.

Talk to the people you are going with beforehand about matters such as discipline. It may be that one family will put up with hours of television watching or that the children have totally different routines, bedtimes, amounts of pocket money. What will you tolerate? One family said, 'We became very worried because Robert copied their son's disgusting behaviour at table, so we went out for a picnic every day.'

Discuss the share of child care and baby-sitting before you embark on the holiday and reach compromises out of the children's hearing. If both families can take their own car, this will give more freedom and privacy.

Sort out in advance the limits and divisions of your finances. Your children will be rather put out watching their friends being treated to water skiing lessons, pony rides, shows and meals out when you cannot afford to splash out.

Finding holiday help

If you do not want to share your holiday with another family, there are other options to relieve you of the 24-hour responsibility.

Grandparents First decide whether you will be able to tolerate one another for a week or two. Will you be spending your time keeping the noise level down? Do you have radically different views about child care, discipline or meal-times? Will they mind staying in to baby-sit while you have some evenings off? How much assistance do you expect from them? Will Granny find it tiring constantly trying to prevent your brood from straying? Remember that this may be the grandparents' holiday too (especially if they are paying their own way), and bear in mind the generation gap.

An extra pair of hands The girl-next-door, a cousin or aunt? You may know someone who dotes on children whom you could take along either at your or their own expense. Try not to choose someone who is totally undomesticated as you do not really want to be cooking a meal for your baby-sitter before setting off for your evening out.

Paid live-in help What would be the cost of taking a paid helper, be it a mother's help or your regular student babysitter? Remember that she will join you at dinner on the nights you stay in. First make it clear what you would expect her to do. Consider her needs too: she will require some privacy, even if you cannot give her a room of her own, and some time off.

Locally arranged help In Britain you should contact the owners of your holiday house for local advice as they may know of a student or housewife who would welcome the job of helping with household chores or with the children. Maid service is often provided in southern European self-catering apartments and villas, or you might be able to hire a full-time helper locally through the tourist office. 'Our holiday to Turkey was made an even greater success by the daily helper who cost us a pittance and occupied Richard, 9 months, whenever we wanted,' said one satisfied mum.

What to Think About Before Booking

Once you have decided where to go, return to your original sources for more details about choices of accommodation. Write to or telephone the proprietors of places where you might stay. Don't be intimidated – they will usually try to help. You will want to know the answers to the following questions, where relevant:

Accommodation   Which floor is it on? Is there a safe lift? Is there a balcony? Is there a separate kitchen which you can shut your toddler out of, rather than just a kitchenette in the corner of the living area? Is there somewhere that parents sharing a bedroom with the children can play cards or read without one or other party emigrating to the bathroom?

Bedrooms   Will you be sharing with your child or children? Think about the pros and cons: older ones will feel that their style is cramped and you may resent your loss of liberty. Younger ones may creep into your bed at midnight or disturb you with snores and snuffles and early morning play. You will have to creep around when you go to bed if you turn in at different times . . . Is this your idea of a restful holiday? But if you do not share a room in a hotel your children may be sleeping way down the corridor and getting up to all sorts of tricks. You don't want to spend the second week of your holiday with Dad sleeping with one child and Mum with the other, following complaints from the neighbours.

Beds   Will everyone have a proper bed, or even a bed of their own? Several tour companies expect children to 'top and tail' in their parents' room in order to qualify for discounts. Do not accept a cot for an over

2 year old (unless absolutely necessary) if you choose a hotel, as the staff may treat your toddler as a baby, travelling free, and will not tidy the cot each day or provide a separate towel.

Washing facilities   Is there a bath? If not, are your children going to enjoy a shower? Are there adequate facilities for washing clothes and, more importantly, drying them? If you are travelling with very young children look for somewhere with a washing machine.

The beach   Is it sand or shingle? Is it clean? Does it shelve steeply into the sea or is it flat with warm shallow pools at low tide? Are there strong currents or tides or other local hazards like jellyfish? Is there equipment on the beach (from sun umbrellas to cafés)? Will you have to pay to use it?

Distances   How far is it to the cycle hire shop or the riding stables? How far to the shops or swimming pool? How far is the beach? How far across the beach to the sea to drag a sailboard or a buggy which will get bogged down in soft sand?

Equipment   Exactly what will be provided? Can you hire tennis rackets or golf clubs? Are there highchairs (and not just one for 20 babies)? Is there a cot and, if so, what style is it and will you have to pay extra? Will bedding and bed-linen be provided?

Hotels   Think about size. Maybe you would prefer one that is not so large that you can't keep an eye on the children, or so small that you get stuck with the only other British couple there with whom you have little in common. Will you be in an annexe? (Ever tried jogging 200 yards up the road between courses to check on your offspring during dinner?) Is there a dining room in the hotel? If not, and you have to go to a restaurant, are your children old enough to have dinner with you at whatever time it is served in that country? Will the hotel serve an early meal for young children or will they have to live on takeaways?

Self-catering   Have you thought carefully about the advantages and disadvantages of different types of apartments, villas and cottages? Flats, closely packed villa complexes, terraced cottages and tents may mean that you will be disturbed by noise and your children may disturb others. Doors and windows will be open most of the time. Can you tolerate a holiday where you may be spending your time controlling the children or feeling guilty, or can you just forget about it? The disadvantages of a complex may be outweighed by the possibility of communal gardens, a swimming pool and other children for yours to play with.

Recreation areas   Is there a garden or terrace where the children can go? Is there play equipment suitable for their age group? Is the playground in the shade?

Convenience and safety   What is the access like? Is there a busy road outside? Are there steps up to the front door or a slope too steep for the double buggy? Is there an unfenced garden, or pond into which your toddler can fall?

Baby-sitting in the evenings. Find out about the kind of service offered. Is it someone listening to the intercom or your phone off the hook? If so, will you remember to replace your phone before you start criticising the unhelpfulness of the receptionist? If the sitter visits your hotel room or chalet, how often is the patrol?

Getting The Best Deal

On the assumption that most people with kids operate on a tight budget, we have tried to identify some of the ways in which you can reduce your costs.

The first rule is – if you have the time and the energy – to compare the prices of all, or at least some, of the operators featuring the same or similar accommodation. This applies wherever you are going, as one operator's mid season may be another's economy season. We heard a sad tale of a family in a Breton gîte who discovered that their semi-detached neighbours, with an extra bedroom, had paid £286 for their fortnight with another company compared with their own bill for £478. They blamed only themselves, and it spoilt their holiday completely. It was no consolation to know that, had they chosen their agency in August, they would have paid £50 less than their neighbours. With small operators, brochures are planned and printed with no idea what the competition is planning to charge.

The second rule is to remember that package deals don't always offer the best value, particularly if you select a smaller hotel or individual self-catering property. For package deals you are paying, sometimes dearly, for the privilege of having the whole holiday arranged for you and for the services of a courier or representative. With cheap plane seats now available to all comers through travel agents you can still benefit from what used to be the exclusive province of the tour operators. There is also a price to be paid for good marketing which lures people into spending more. Companies like English Country Cottages or Vacances, with their excellent and most attractive brochures, lure people into renting properties in England and in France which would be significantly cheaper rented through a small ad or the Gîtes de France organisation. When you book through such firms you pay for the production of those enticing brochures as well as the costs of their advertising. They are not cheating you, just offering a service that plenty of people are prepared to pay for.

One of the greatest savings for the independent traveller is avoiding the blatant profiteering by many tour companies at the expense of families in high season. If you choose to take a holiday in a hotel in Britain, the child who shares with parents in a normal twin room is either offered free accommodation, charged an amount to cover the hire of a bed and linen or is offered an all-in rate appropriate to the accommodation provided and the expected consumption of food. If you take an independent hotel holiday abroad you would book a three-bedded room costing 15% to 30% more than a twin and pay for travel and meals as taken. But if you take a package tour to the Mediterranean the chances are that you will share a normal twin room with a 'put-you-up' crammed into one corner and, in high season, be given a 20% discount at best and no discount at worst . . . and then usually only until the child's twelfth birthday.

In our view, if the cost of an ordinary double room makes up one third of the adult holiday price then the discount should be one third. In practice, of course, with large firms, that discount is spread over the year so that out of season a lot of money is 'lost' giving away free aircraft seats and 50% discounts. If the cost of the child's holiday looks as though it will be more than the full cost of the flight, the transfer, the smaller portions of food, hire of bed and bed linen and a contribution to overheads – and you do not get a proper three-bedded room at the end of it – think seriously about going independently. Why not use a travel agent with a computer link to Touropa, which offers direct booking to over a thousand hotels and apartment complexes in Europe?

Free child places on package holidays

Old hands will not need to be told that those heavily promoted 'free' holidays are limited in number, usually only available in off-peak weeks and most are only for one child sharing a room with two adults. Two parents and two children will only qualify by squeezing themselves into one room – fine in some hotels but means two children sharing a bed in others (heed the dire warnings in the Intasun and Thomson brochures).

If you choose a self-catering package, a 'free' holiday usually raises the price of the package for the rest of the party, so is not 'free' at all. However, they can be tremendously valuable for two parents with one child and of some value to the family with three children sharing a room.

Undoubtedly the secret of securing a free holiday is to book really early. A high proportion of free holidays are taken by repeat bookers making their reservation long before the brochures are in the travel agents for all to see. This is risky as you may not have a confirmed price for your own holiday nor will you be able to scrutinise the travel schedules in advance – you could find yourself on the dreaded night flights. In order to be an equally early bird you will have to decide a year in advance where you want to go (from the previous year's brochures).

Some companies have taken to guaranteeing unconditional free holidays, subject to the usual restrictions, to all families booking before a certain date in December or January. You might fare better with these companies as their policy is only revealed on publication of the brochures. Most qualifying accommodation offered by specialists with relatively small programmes, like Sunmed's 'Go Greek' could well be booked up before the closing date of the offer, if past years are any guide.

If you are going well out of season it is never too late to enquire about free holidays. We had a report of a family getting a free holiday in Majorca in January at a few weeks' notice.

Those securing a free holiday do not usually pay airport taxes or fuel surcharges (when they arise) but will have to pay a full deposit on booking which is then allowed for in the calculation of the final invoice. But do look out for one or two of the minor companies who slap on extra charges. Usually free children have to pay an insurance premium.

Free children's holidays in Britain

These do not have the same cash value as the much-hyped promotional deals for overseas holidays, as any travel included is worth very little . . . if you go by train, you will presumably be using a Family Rail Card.

Many chains of hotels accommodate the kids at no charge. But you will have to pay for the meals they eat, which somewhat detracts from the value of the offer. For a bargain, try a Crest Weekend, when up to three children can have their own room at no overnight charge.

Your best bet for a true free holiday is the Holiday Centres, with special mention going to Pontin's who offer two free places to a family of four out of season provided the children are under 10 . . . and this can mean full board for them all for a total £160 for a week.

Child discounts on holidays abroad

Child discounts are fairly clear in most of the brochures, although wading through all of those featuring the same hotel can be a mammoth and complex task. This is made worse by some companies offering as standard what others charge extra for, like airport taxes, a balcony or full board.

The range of discounts for children sharing with two adults is staggering with some companies offering good discounts (which we would define as 30% or more) throughout the season, while others give no discount at all in the school summer holidays. Some offer a discount for a second child sharing with two adults while others offer them nothing despite the fact that there may be no proper bed for the second child. In this instance you may be only marginally worse off if you pay for both children in full and put them in a separate room.

Most companies offer no discount to children in their own room. The few that do are those which offer a blanket discount to all children (see below) and those which give something off for kids sharing with one full price holidaymaker (see page 127 under One Parent Holidays). If you have three children, then usually only the third will qualify for a discount, but that would be at the best rate with every company.

However, some companies offer a discount to all those under a certain age, regardless of room arrangements. These include Thomson (10% off all holidays at all times); careful scrutiny of the brochures may reward you with similar bargains. The prize for the best deal has to go to a very small company called Cricketer Holidays who allow approximately 20%

off all season for children from 2 to 18 years provided they share a room with one or two others, i.e. each of three children receive the discount. Perhaps others can be persuaded to follow their lead.

If you have one or more child over 11 years, do not despair totally. Operators are slowly realising that there is little sense in an arbitrary cut-off at the twelfth birthday where charter flights are involved, and you will find some price reductions for older children. Some are better than others with our special accolade going to Falcon Family Holidays who recognise that kids are kids until they are 16 and nearly ready to go off on beach holidays on their own. Beach Villas, Citalia, Club Cantabrica, Cosmos, Enterprise, Global, Intasun Apartments and Lancaster all offer some sort of discount for 12 to 16s. And how about the small Cricketer Holidays or Travel Club of Upminster who realise that many families not only still have dependent 18 and 19 year olds but that they may want to take them on holiday and get a discount?

Child discounts on holidays in Britain

As the fixed price of travel is rarely included in holidays near home the discounts are generally better, although there are few to be had on self-catering holidays. If you choose a hotel, guest house or holiday centre you will find that cut price holidays can be offered up to about 16 years. There are no significant variations with season, and cheaper holidays for the young are offered right through July and August.

Infants on air packages

IATA regulations allow children under 2 to be carried on a parent's lap without paying for a seat. They are, therefore, normally taken for a nominal amount (about £10) if you are travelling by charter flight, although a few companies take infants at no charge. You will normally have to pay for food and cot rental, as appropriate, when you get there, which can cost up to £5 a day. At this price you may be tempted to pass your under 2 as older in order to qualify for a free holiday – which certainly cannot be against IATA regulations.

However, we do know that if you attempt to pass off a child over 2 years as an infant you will be charged in full if you are discovered, normally losing any entitlement to child discounts and possibly being charged for the additional administration required. One mother who took her daughter as an infant, a week after her second birthday, told us that she spent her whole holiday in a cold sweat fearing detection.

If you are travelling by scheduled flight you will be charged a minimum of 10% of the adult fare.

Other savings

If you are booking a package holiday through a travel agent there are other special offers around which could save you hundreds of pounds, particularly on out-of-season breaks:

Cheap fares to the airport by British Rail. These may not be worth having if you already have a Family Rail Card.

Free parking at the airport is quite commonly offered, which can be worth up to £30 for a fortnight's trip.

Free hotel accommodation at the airport for those taking early morning flights, as do, for example, Thomas Cook on their Winter programme in 1986/7.

Free car-hire is often featured by the more up-market hotels in popular spots in the winter months, e.g. at numerous hotels in Majorca. This can range from just one day's hire to a whole fortnight's, but you will have to pay an insurance premium. You may also find that some airlines to North America offer free or cheap car-hire as an incentive.

Free or special rate insurance may be offered by some travel agents (e.g. W H Smith in 1986) which could be worth up to around £30 per person.

Early booking discounts, which vary from £10 vouchers redeemable at the rate of one per booking form to £25 off per head for those booking before a certain date (others might call these a late booking penalty). Some even offer 10% off all holidays for next year provided you book and pay in full within one month of returning from this year's holiday.

A cut price or even free second holiday may be offered to those booking before a certain date, as an incentive to book early. Rank Holidays (OSL, Ellerman, Blue Sky, etc.) offer, for example, a spring holiday at Butlins from £5 a week, self-catering or a weekend in London at a Rank hotel.

Lastly, see if you can find a travel agent who will give you a discount on your holiday. Some are happy to offer 5% off holidays booked by individual members of a club or association. You may belong to an organisation with such an arrangement. If not, now is the time to do a deal on behalf of your sports club, staff association, union branch or even PTA. If the agents estimate that business will double among your members then it will surely be to their benefit.

What it Will Cost

The cost of the holiday will depend on where you go, when you go and what sort of child discount you managed to secure. When you sit down to book your holiday and cost it out run through the following points:

The travel agent or tour operator's bill

Calculating the basic cost of the holiday could need a degree in mathematics with some companies – perhaps good reason for renting a holiday cottage for which you pay a simple weekly rental! The bill could include the following:

The basic holiday price after deduction of child discounts.

Room supplements for single occupation, a bath, sea-view, balcony or cot.

Under occupation supplements if you have chosen an inclusive villa or apartment holiday with air or coach travel.

Flight supplements for day-time departures or for travel from your local airport.

Airport taxes which are payable for everyone of 2 years and over. Most large companies include these in the holiday price.

VAT which is not always shown in the basic price for holidays in Britain. The worst offenders are the Activity Holiday specialists.

Insurance for you, your possessions and your car, including vehicle retrieval policy (e.g. AA 5 star or Europ Assistance).

Before you go

You may need to incur the following expenses:

Passports   It costs £15 for each person for a full passport, whether or not it carries the names of their children, and £3 to add a child to an existing adult's document.

Vaccinations if required. For example, a shot of cholera vaccine required by visitors to Morocco can cost £5 for administration plus the cost of the prescription, meaning a bill of around £25 for a family of four.

Getting to your resort

If you plan an air holiday you will need to look at these costs before booking as they may affect your choice of flight time or departure airport. For example, it may be more economic to drive to a London airport and pay for parking than to pay the, say, £14 supplement to fly from Manchester for each of four people.

Cost of getting to the airport, parking there and an overnight stay en route, if necessary. Even if you are travelling by train you may still need a taxi to the station.

Petrol and the general running costs of the car if you are driving to your resort. Do not forget motorway tolls if you are going to France, Spain or Italy or the one-off charge levied for use of the Swiss system.

Cost of ferries   They may be included in your holiday price if you are going to the Continent but it is easy to forget that a trip to the Isle of Wight, for example, will cost nearly £40 if you take the car.

When you get there

Always ensure that you have access to more funds (in travellers cheques or Eurocheques) than you think you may need, to allow for emergencies such as doctor's bills.

Meals   Your budget will obviously have to reflect the meal plan included in your holiday price. If you are self-catering allow for a few meals out or takeaways. For those with some meals provided, how much it will cost to feed the family at lunch-time or for an evening meal in a café or restaurant every day? Can you picnic or is it more sensible to have hot meals every day? Do not forget to budget for the cost of wine, beers or soft drinks with pre-paid hotel meals: the hotel bar bill at the end of the week, although generally payable by credit card, can be the bitterest part of the holiday.

Deposit against possible damage to the property. This can be an unexpected drain on your reserves of cash. You may have to travel with your wallet bulging with francs or pesetas so that you can meet the cash deposit of, say, £150 required to secure the keys of your gîte or apartment.

Local taxes may be payable, like the recently introduced 'Taxe de sejour' in France, which is up to 30p per head per day.

Linen hire if you choose a caravan or holiday centre.

Cot hire if not paid for on the original invoice.

Extra charges for electricity, gas, firewood or cleaning if you are self-catering.

Excursions and entrance fees for the whole family. If you are thinking about going on all-day coach excursions then a family of four will need at least £50 for each one planned, so you will probably be better off hiring a car for the day. If you think it could rain during your holiday you will need to plan for more outings than if you are heading for sunnier climes.

The cost of activities like riding, boat hire, tennis court rental or cycling. These can mount up, particularly if one of you needs instruction. There would be no problem for a potential windsurfer to get through £50 for five lessons and board rental for practice, while young equestrians could spend the same amount in rather fewer hours. If you plan to go skiing, extras can mount up to over £200 a head for a fortnight.

Car hire if you need transport once you get there. In addition to the basic hire charge you may need to add VAT (or the equivalent, which in Spain can add one third to the price). Insurance and petrol will bump the whole cost up to £20 to £30 per day.

Pocket money for those who have not saved up enough during the year.

Getting home again

If you have any money left you will need it for:

Drinks and snacks If you are not self-catering it may be difficult to take a picnic on the return leg.

Fares home from the airport, if any.

Duty Free goods Remember that under 16s do not get liquor and tobacco allowances.

How to Travel

The journey will be the important start and end of your holiday and an aspect you may have to consider when you book your accommodation. You may also need to speculate in general terms about how much luggage you need to take for a family for a fortnight.

Plan your schedule well bearing in mind any time changes. On a long journey, you may have the choice of travelling by day or night. Do you really mind getting up at 4 am in order to check in early enough for a so-called 'day-time flight' at 7 am? Remember, however, that your chosen schedule can be broken very easily at the whim of your tour operator or the airline.

Your child's routine needs to be considered. For example, some night ferries do not leave until very late and a ferry which docks at 7 am means that you have to rise at 6 am – and that would be 5 am 'stomach time' on the outward leg to Europe, due to the time difference. Don't worry about oversleeping, the crew will see you are awake in time to get to the car deck.

Think about transfers on a journey. If you want to go to Paxos in the Greek islands, for example, there could be a six hour wait in Corfu Town and then a three hour ferry crossing. The journey might be so exhausting for you all that you will feel it was hardly worth the effort, particularly on the way home.

Choose your route with care. Calculate how far you are prepared to drive in Britain and abroad and weigh the cost against convenience.

Splitting the family up for the journey is favoured by some. Dad and the eldest go by car with all the gear, whilst Mum and Granny take the younger ones by train or plane. You may avoid travel sickness and possible personality clashes, and you can take more people and clobber.

After all, how many have a car large enough for their own family, Granny and the bicycles as well as the buggy and travel cot?

If you have chosen a holiday in Britain, you will usually take your car if you have one (although possibly not for a city holiday); otherwise you will have the choice of train, coach and plane for longer journeys.

When travelling over the Channel the options become a little more confusing, particularly if you are going between 400 and 800 miles from the Channel ports. Here we outline some of the pros and cons of each mode of transport to help you in your choice:

Going by car

Having a car ensures flexibility to go when and where you want and to take more things with you. The main problem for many families is space; the car which is fine for running round town may simply not be large enough or reliable enough to take overseas. After all, a family of five going on a charter flight can take 165 lb (75 kg) of luggage, perhaps more than the old jalopy.

If you want to go on holiday by car remember the additional expenses over and above the petrol (see page 27).

When you plan how far to drive, do not be too ambitious with your mileage schedules. The distance you can travel obviously depends on whether you will be able to use motorways, how many drivers there are and whether you hit the big traffic jams (any Saturday in July and August in Britain and, in France, the first weekend in July and the last in August).

Air travel

A little planning early on can ease the problems of air travelling provided your tour company does not consolidate the flights or change flight times 'due to circumstances beyond our control'.

Departure airport Look at the economics and convenience of travelling from your local airport; if you live north of London and want to take a flight from London you may be wiser to choose a tour company with Luton or Stansted flights. If you particularly want to go on a holiday served only by flights from Gatwick look into the cost of taking a commuter or shuttle flight from your local airport at either end of your holiday (if you go British Caledonian then you can ask for a Mother's Assistant to help with the flight transfer).

Destination airport   There may be a choice of airports serving your destination, so weigh up the pros and cons of the alternatives with reference to transfer times and flight schedules. Remember that different companies may serve the same resort via different airports. The main examples are to be found in the skiing programmes, although they do occur elsewhere. If you choose a small destination airport you will almost certainly have to travel to London to catch the flight.

Day of the week   If you can be flexible choose to travel on a week day: you may not only save money but also have a more congenial flight time from a less crowded airport.

Time of day   Night flights, despite their economy, are not recommended for families. Imagine dealing with your tired, fractious offspring from 3 am until the cafés open for breakfast, and keeping them in the same clothes until you can book into your accommodation at midday! Similarly, try and arrange your return flight so that it fits in with the time you have to check out of your accommodation. One family said, 'We decided to hire a car for the last day so that we could prevent the long wait until our 8 pm departure becoming a dreadful anti-climax to the holiday. It had the added advantage of providing somewhere to store our paraphernalia, including wet swimming things.'

As far as cost is concerned, if you travel by charter flight children normally pay a full, or virtually full, fare once they are over 2 years old when, according to IATA regulations, they should occupy their own seat; infants sitting on their parents' knees go free. Those travelling by scheduled airline normally pay 10% between birth and 2 years and 50% of the adult fare between 2 and 12 years.

Coach travel

Coach travel has much improved in recent years in comfort and in facilities. Many have loos and provide refreshments, and you can enjoy fabulous views from a double decker or watch a video show. Sleeper coaches with bunks are an alternative for long distance overnight travel. It is also a very economic way to travel. We know of one family who took their children to Greece – a three-day coach journey – and thoroughly enjoyed it. You may think they were mad, but it does prove that it's possible!

Coach tour holidays, moving from one hotel to another and generally appealing to older travellers, are really not suitable for children of any age. They will be frustrated enough by the restriction imposed by the odd day tour you might choose to take during your holiday, or that inevitable coach journey which follows your flight on any package holiday.

If you want to travel by scheduled coach service in Britain you will find that there are various child discounts according to carrier. The largest, National Coaches, take under 5s free provided each child travels with a full fare-paying passenger, while 5 to 16 year olds travel at approximately two thirds of normal fare.

Train travel

Undoubtedly, for straightforward travel between two centres there is little to beat the train in terms of speed and comfort; the children can get up and move around, everyone gets a good view out of the window, and you can buy drinks and snacks on major routes. While most publicity is centred on cut-backs in service, the cross-country routes so valuable to the holiday-maker continue unnoticed – invaluable for those with children who find changing at Birmingham New Street so much simpler than crossing London from one terminus to another.

British Rail allows under 5s to travel free, with half-fare up to 16 years. It's sensible to check out all the alternative saver fares and particularly the seasonal specials like 'Kids Out, Quids In'. Costs can also be markedly reduced by the various railcards available which entitle holders to further reductions. The most important of these is the £15 annual Family Rail Card which allows up to four adults to travel at one third off with up to four children paying £1 each. At least one child must travel with the party, so even if you have only under 5s one of them will be charged. But there are restrictions, so watch out if you plan to use it for a weekend away or to travel on a Saturday during August.

If you are planning a trip to Europe you can invest £5 in a Rail Europ card. A party of three or more people living at the same address can claim discounts while 4 to 11 year olds pay half the reduced adult fare. The cards are available from principal BR stations and are valid for a year.

Book seats and/or sleeping accommodation well ahead for the principal holiday weekends. Sleeping compartments in Britain are for one (in first class) or two (in second class). You will need a ticket for each berth used, even for under 5s in addition to the £15 charge for the berth. If you decide to sleep on the train on the Continent then only under 4s travel free. You will normally be allocated a couchette in a six-berth cabin with total strangers who may not be pleased by your children's antics. For your children, it makes a thrilling start to the holiday: 'Catriona and Siobhan look forward to the train journey, which takes us on our annual trip to Dundee, almost more than to the holiday itself,' says one mother.

Motorail

If you are planning a long journey in Britain or France this is the one way you can ease your journey, although it is an expensive option. It's particularly valuable if there is only one driver, if one of you is worried about driving on strange roads or if you are concerned about the reliability of your car. Think through the economics carefully allowing for savings in petrol, wear and tear, motorway tolls and overnight accommodation. Unless you own what the Americans call a 'gas guzzler' that clocks up only 10 miles to the gallon, it will still be more expensive than driving, but you will arrive at your destination quicker and feeling much more refreshed. However, check the timetables carefully as services are often restricted to certain periods in high season.

Ferries and hovercraft

The ferry companies are in the middle of a programme of massive refurbishment or replacement of ships so that you should find larger,

Child Discounts and Fare Structure on Ferries

Operator	Child Discounts	Qualifying Ages	Special Family Fares	Notes
B & I Line	Free or 50% off depending on season	5–15	'Weekenders' or '7 day mid-week'	2 or 4 berth cabins available.
Brittany Ferries	50% off	4–13	No	Under 4s requiring a berth or reclining seat must hold a ticket.
Channel Island Ferries	50% off	4–13	'Midweek Family Fares'	Whole cabins available.
DFDS	50% off	4–15	No	Under 4s requiring a berth or reclining seat must hold a ticket.
Hoverspeed	50% off	4–13	No	—
Isle of Man Steam Packet	50% off 20% off	5–15 Student	No No	— —
North Sea Ferries	50% off	2–13	Budget fares in special cabins	Obligatory to take a berth for under 14s.
Norway Line	50% off	4–15	No	Under 4s requiring a berth must hold a ticket.

Olau-Line	Free Mon–Fri daytime or 45% off; other times 20% off	4–13 14–17	No No	2 or 4 berth cabins available.
Olsen	50% off	4–15	No	Under 4s requiring a berth must hold a ticket.
Sally Line	First child free, others 50% off	4–13	No	—
Sealink: Eire	Free or 33–50% off depending on season	4–13	'Weekend Family Fares' and '7 day mid-week Family Fare'	—
Sealink: France	50% off	4–13	No	Where berths available, a 2 or 4 berth cabin can be booked.
Sealink: Holland	Free on day crossings, or 50% off on night crossings	4–13	No	Under 4s requiring a berth must hold a ticket.
Sealink: Channel Islands	50% off	5–15	'Family Moneysavers'	2 and 4 berth Economy cabins available.
Sealink: Ulster	48% off	5–15	No	—
Townsend Thoresen	50% off	4–13	No	2 and 4 berth cabins available.

more comfortable and cheerful vessels with better facilities than in the past.

When you choose your route remember that the longer ferry crossings may not be so expensive once you have allowed for petrol and overnight stops. For example, there can be great savings in motoring hours if you go to Brittany or western France via St Malo, Cherbourg, Caen or Roscoff. Book early for peak travel times (the most expensive!) and if you require a cabin as there are not enough to go round on most ferries. Reclining seats are far from ideal for kids.

Going by Hovercraft to France is quick, but you are limited by the routes available. In bad weather you can be subjected to a very rough and unpleasant crossing, and in appalling conditions your flight may be cancelled.

As far as cost goes, getting the best ferry deal is another exercise which will take a whole weekend of poring over brochures. You have to balance the cost of the car (and trailer/caravan which may go free on some sailings) with the passenger fares, child discounts and regulations on occupation of berths. In 1986 the picture looked like the table on pages 34–35.

If you travel with under 14s you might consider joining the Sealink Commodore Club; for £1 you get membership plus four free non-transferable child-rate tickets for use during that year. You only need one round trip to save at least £10.

When to Book

There is no doubt that the only way to get exactly what you want in the way of accommodation, dates and discounts is to book early, even if you do not feel like planning the next holiday just a few months after returning from the last one.

How early is early? That depends on when you want to go and the type of holiday. The most popular holiday cottages at the water's edge in Cornwall, for example, will be booked for August at least a year in advance while gîtes for the same period are reserved well before Christmas. Early bookers get the best rooms, the best cottages and the best value. Early bookers too will often be repeat bookers who are not waiting for brochures to make up their minds.

The one case in Britain where early booking is not essential is when seeking a site for your tent. You will probably find spaces even in August.

As far as scheduled transport is concerned, you have virtually nothing to lose if later you want to change your route or timings, so you should always book your travel when you book your accommodation. Peak ferry sailings and motorail are usually the first to be booked up, while train seats and scheduled plane seats can be left quite late, although at least three weeks' notice is advisable.

And what about last minute bargains? These are definitely for the childless! Remember how difficult it will be to get four or five seats on the same flight, let alone two rooms in the same hotel.

Holidays in the British Isles

Self-Catering

Self-catering holidays are very popular, perhaps because parents feel that, in a cottage or flat, they can avoid the strain of imposing high standards of behaviour on their children. And you can take the dog! If you have self-catered before, much of what we say will seem obvious, but going to self-catering accommodation for the first time, even without children, can be rather a shock. It is the way of holidaying that most new parents think they can manage, and although most comments we received indicated many people enjoyed their holiday, they pointed out various pitfalls which are not unique to self-catering but deserve a mention:

● The property will not necessarily be the same as a house you borrow from friends; the furniture may be old and uncomfortable. The cheaper the house the more likely it is to have that nasty damp smell. So look for accommodation that has been individually inspected or conforms to the standards of the tourist boards.

● One of the drawbacks of this type of holiday for children could be the lack of company. Unless you are sharing your accommodation with (or are adjacent to) another family, you may be quite isolated. The solution might be to look at a purpose-built complex, often known as a holiday village, or to select a cottage in a group with others.

● You will be going to unknown territory which isn't child proofed to the standard your child requires. 'Joanna threw half a dozen eggs individually to the floor from an easily openable fridge at her temporary home . . . at home, they would have been in a locked pantry.'

● You will normally be expected to leave the property in a clean and tidy state. So, not only will you be rushing to pack up and go by 10 am on the last day, but you will also be dashing around with the vacuum cleaner and duster.

Individual and groups of self-catering flats and houses

These can be found through a variety of sources. Try the following:

Brochures either from a travel agent, including Blake's *Country and Seaside Holidays* and *Character Cottages*, or from the Tourist Boards for Scotland and Wales.

Directories　There are various directories on the market, such as the *Good Holiday Cottage Guide* (especially good for groups of cottages), the *Farm Holiday Guides* (which cover rural houses as well as catered holidays), *Cade's Self-Catering Holiday Guide* and the AA's *Holiday Homes, Cottages and Apartments in Britain*.

Letting agents　The larger regional letting agents advertise in the Sunday papers. To take just one example, *English Country Cottages*, *Welsh Country Cottages* and *Country Cottages in Scotland* are the three regional brochures of English Country Cottages Ltd, which are clear, with colour pictures and state whether baby-sitting and cots are available. They feature several groups of cottages including one with an aviary, a tree-house and a playground for the 10 properties. You might also look at the *Summer Cottages* brochure which you can buy from larger newsagents.

Local tourist offices and local estate agents. If you know where you want to go, telephone for a list of local cottages or landlords.

National Trust, Forestry Commission and Landmark Trust cottages and houses, often in interesting converted buildings (including gothic follies and old school houses). They are invariably in beauty spots and get booked up early.

Private ads in periodicals and newspapers, in particular, *The Observer*, *The Sunday Times* and *The Lady*. Also try your staff magazine, or your local NCT newsletter if you want something oriented towards small children. These sources usually bring you into direct contact with the owner and you can ask for photographs and layout plans.

Purpose-built 'holiday villages'

These are featured in many of the brochures and range from the Scandinavian log cabins of the Forestry Commission to the chalet-style villages from Hoseasons, which only need entertainment programmes to count as holiday centres. (See that section.) They probably will have some central facilities, such as a games room or a launderette.

You could look at:

B & I Line's *Holidays in Ireland* which offers attractive groups of cottages all over the south and west of Ireland.

Blake's *Country and Seaside Holidays* features in their well set out brochure some groups of lodges and apartments amongst their individual cottages.

BUAC (British Universities Accommodation Consortium) offer self-catering flats and houses during the university vacations on several campuses including York, Aberystwyth and St Andrews. Although not purpose-built for holiday-makers and sometimes not by the sea, they might be an interesting alternative.

Cabin Holidays aim to provide high quality cabins in beautiful locations in Scotland, Wales and Cornwall.

CIE Tours *Ireland Holidays* offer five holiday villages in western Ireland.

The Forestry Commission's *Get Away To It All* features attractive cabin complexes in Argyllshire, Perthshire, Cornwall and the North York Moors.

Hoseason's *Holiday Homes* offers complexes with communal facilities amongst the holiday centres.

Isle of Man Steam Packet's *Seaways* offers five of the island's finest self-catering establishments.

Sealink's *Experience Ireland* features six villages in the west of Ireland.

Special facilities for children

There may not be much apart from a swing in the garden unless you opt for a holiday village where you should at least find a play area and may find much more. If you want more entertainment, look at the Holiday Centres section.

Taking babies and toddlers

Cots are normally available, although some may have seen better days. Some guides and brochures indicate whether baby-sitting may be available. These include Jonathan Lewis's *Family Holiday Guide*, the AA's *Holiday Homes, Cottages and Apartments in Britain*, and the *Summer Cottages, Character Cottages* and the three *English Country Cottages Ltd* brochures. Baby-sitting is not normally available in holiday villages as there is no willing owner anywhere near.

Self-catering equipment

You will need to take:

For the whole family
- mugs (seldom provided)
- your favourite knife or any other essential kitchen gadget
- wet weather indoor pursuits

- picnic things
- bed linen
- towels
- tea towels, cleaning materials, toilet paper, etc.
- your basics for catering, e.g. tea, flour and sufficient food for your first meal and breakfast the next day.

For small children
- plastic feeding equipment (all breakages have to be paid for)
- extra teaspoons
- any favourite branded item that may be difficult to obtain in isolated parts of Britain
- cot linen.

Cost

An individual cottage may cost between £300 and £1000 per week in high season. Cabins, apartments and chalets in holiday complexes, without ferry crossings, will cost £200–£300. In Ireland, the cost for two weeks will be about £300–£400 and on the Isle of Man £600, both including the cost of the ferry. You will normally have to pay for gas and electricity as consumed and any breakages.

Child discounts are not normally available as the accommodation is priced per unit. For the Irish holidays, the price is calculated on the number of adults in the car and under 16s cost nothing.

Hotels

There is little problem finding hotels where children are welcome. The information is freely available in directories and brochures and also by telephone. Although phoning a large hotel may simply put you in touch with the duty receptionist, a call to a small hotel or guest house will allow you to contact the proprietor direct.

Numerous families have told us about hotel holidays in Britain. Many had chosen hotels which catered especially for families. The success of these for the children was undoubted as they played all day with others of their own age, but many parents were less enthusiastic. They complained about dull food, far from luxurious bedrooms without even a television, and dreary bars.

The most consistent complaint concerned the child-oriented food, which meant fish fingers, chips and beans followed by ice cream. The children were in seventh heaven but the parents were definitely fretting that their youngsters would go home and refuse healthy home cooking.

Others were unhappy that advertised playrooms 'were passage ways from one part of the hotel to another.' There were also complaints about the play equipment as it sometimes includes space invader machines. Table tennis for the teens is often mixed with equipment for tiny tots. Baby-listening services also came in for criticism with several families commenting that intercoms were playing to unmanned reception desks. It should be emphasised that these problems were not universal and were less likely to apply at the more expensive end of the market.

Despite the fact that some hotels did not satisfy in all respects, many people had a good holiday and said that their children were able to meet others of their own age, and parents felt less conscious of their noisy or crying offspring.

Comments we received suggest that a small hotel without any special facilities might sometimes be a better bet than those with all the trimmings. The proprietor may be happy to baby-sit or to serve food to order even if your family is the only one in residence.

Accommodation

Identifying the right hotel for you will, to some extent, depend on where you want to go. If you have a firm plan to take your holiday in a particular area, contact the local tourist office for their promotional literature and then phone the hotels individually for further information or leaflets.

An easier route is to consult one or more of the books which list hotels and carry their advertisements. Try a general directory like *Where to Stay – England, Hotels* or *Scotland – Where to Stay, Hotels and Guesthouses*, published by the Tourist Boards (using symbols to designate that children are welcome) or one of the specialists for family holidays including:

England's Seaside, English Tourist Board. This is a comprehensive listing of English Tourist Board hotel and guesthouse subscribers by the sea who welcome children; like other ETB publications, entries are in a classified format so you can take in facilities and cost at a glance. Each hotel must sign a declaration indicating that staff welcome families and must offer feeding, sleeping and laundry facilities appropriate to those travelling with very young children.

Children Welcome, a Herald Holiday Handbook. Essentially a resort guide which carries advertisements for hotels in England, Wales and Scotland.

Jonathan Lewis's Family Holiday Guide, another guide to resorts with advertisements and carrying a classified list of those hotels choosing to pay for an entry. Limited entries for Scotland and Wales.

Family Welcome Guide, formerly the *Peaudouce Guide*. This is closer to a 'Good Food Guide' in format, and hotels listed do not pay for their entry; the number of hotels is relatively limited and they do tend to be expensive.

If you prefer to book your holiday through a travel agent you will find a host of brochures featuring holidays in the Channel Islands, Ireland and the Isle of Man, for which you may need a travel-inclusive package.

The area brochures, compiled by tourist boards or a consortium of towns, are marketing their district as well as their accommodation. They vary considerably in terms of the amount of information they provide concerning family holidays, so you or your travel agent may still have to do further investigative work.

Travel agents also carry brochures for the chains of hotels; four groups have hotels specifically aimed at holidaymakers with children and you may find something suitable among these:

Butlin's Holiday Hotels in Blackpool, Brighton, Llandudno, Margate and Scarborough. These offer family fun although no under 9s are accepted at Scarborough and Blackpool, while under 4s are excluded from Llandudno.

Ladbroke Hotels designate three as 'Holiday Hotels'; these are more comfortable versions of their holiday centres and are located in Torbay, Bournemouth and Aviemore.

Mount Charlotte Hotels include three, at Bude, Llanwrtyd Wells and Portpatrick, which are designated as 'Family Holiday Hotels' with children's entertainment and good facilities and equipment for babies and toddlers.

THF welcome children at all their hotels, but designate eight as 'Family Favourites'. These include six hotels near the sea at Christchurch, Exmouth, Padstow, Paignton, Weston-super-Mare and Ventnor and two inland at Pitlochry and Windermere. These offer games rooms, playgrounds, swimming pools, and most of them have a crèche.

Special faclilities for children

Most family-oriented hotels offer facilities and equipment for children's entertainment: many have swimming pools, although generally out of doors and not necessarily heated. You will also find playground equipment and an indoor playroom or games room with table tennis, board games and probably electronic games. A high proportion of bedrooms will fit in a whole family or inter-connecting rooms will be available. Early meals are usually served, although a significant proportion will expect the whole family to sit down together at 6 pm. An evening baby-listening service is usually offered, normally of the intercom type.

Going with babies and toddlers

Family hotels will welcome you and your tots with open arms. You will be safe if you choose a Family hotel listed in *England's Seaside* as these hotels must provide cots and cot linen, high chairs, washing and drying facilities, bottle warming and food preparation facilities in order to qualify for inclusion in the directory. You will also find that a number of hotels have a crèche or playgroup facility.

The Cost

The cost of this type of holiday is quite variable. You can go to one of the THF hotels or the highly acclaimed Saunton Sands or Knoll House, where children's facilities are wonderful, and pay up to £300 per week per adult for a full board holiday. And if you choose a five star hotel like the Imperial at Torquay it will cost about £500! Or you can select one of the many independent hotels listed in the guides where the cost of a half-board holiday will range from £60 per head for a room without private facilities.

Child discounts vary greatly from hotel to hotel; some offer free holidays to children sharing with their parents, but their meals have to be paid for, while others charge a percentage of the adult price, often with several price bands depending on age. Adulthood is generally taken to be 14 years but if you look carefully you will find discounts for children up to 16.

Holiday Centres

The term 'Holiday Centre' covers an enormous range of camps, clubs and villages. Some are almost indistinguishable from family hotels while others might be called caravan parks or chalet parks by the uninitiated. For most of us our conception will be dominated by television images of Butlin's with up to 11,000 happy campers having Fun.

In the holiday centres of the 1980s you will stay in independent accommodation with central facilities, including a restaurant and bar or club room and usually a swimming pool, playground and other sports facilities. There is normally some sort of free entertainment in the evening but there are not always organised daytime activites.

Reports suggested that children had a wonderful time at a holiday centre while the parents had mixed feelings. Adults complained about standards of comfort and particularly about the food and the size of the accommodation. 'We didn't have enough space when it rained to stay in our chalet and amuse ourselves,' said one family. Of course, the size of your accommodation varies from centre to centre and on whether or not you opt for a catered arrangement. One family we know of took the opportunity to lose their children all day to the Redcoats at Butlin's while they lost themselves in the mountains of North Wales, and in the evening were able to make themselves a quiet dinner in the chalet while their children slept off the excesses of the day. The younger members of another family enthused over their holiday at Pontin's in Paignton where they opted out of the country and coastal walks (which their parents enjoyed) in favour of the organised activities.

Accommodation

Today holiday centres such as Butlin's are trying hard to shed their 1960s image of garish fun-palaces with endless messages over the tannoy system and Redcoats who entertain from morning until midnight. At Butlin's (and Pontin's and Warner as well) you will, however, still find endless well organised entertainment for the children, but nowadays the emphasis tends to be on sport. Heated swimming pools with slides and waves are increasingly featured as the centre-piece, with a trend towards covered all-weather sub-tropical versions like that at Butlin's at Minehead now designated 'Somerwest World'.

At the other end of the scale you can stay in self-catering chalets or caravan parks like those offered by Haven, with central facilities like a swimming pool, bar and restaurant but little organised entertainment.

You can choose between a self-catering or catered holiday, with the options varying from centre to centre even within one company. With a half- or full-board holiday you will find that the large, noisy cafeterias have at many centres been replaced by smaller restaurants, some with waitress service. Children's food is, needless to say, of the chips and beans variety.

The standard of accommodation will vary with the price; at the top end of the market are the 'County Suites' at Butlin's or the Warner Club Hotels, both of which offer the standards of a modern hotel room with colour TV and en-suite bathroom. At the bottom end it might be a cramped, elderly, pre-fabricated chalet with peeling paint and no shower room, although this is now rare. Caravan accommodation, using high quality modern vans, is available from most companies while Ladbroke also offer the economic option of 'Supertents'. Standards of service are equally variable: some companies provide linen, tea-making facilities and a daily cleaning service, even for self-caterers, while some provide none of these although linen can be hired.

If you choose to self-cater the accommodation is generally more spacious and you will have a proper kitchen and living area, although this may double as a second or third bedroom. Like self-catering flats or cottages anywhere you will have to take your own soap, towels and tea cloths and pay for the gas and electricity consumed.

Butlin's operate six Holiday Centres in Minehead, Bognor, Skegness, Pwllheli (North Wales), Barry Island (South Wales) and Ayr, all next to a beach. There is self-catering or half-board at most centres, although if you have an under-2 you must take the former. At Ayr the arrangements may differ slightly. Butlin's offer the ultimate in free entertainment with full scale funfairs and free high quality rides and evening entertainment by nationally known TV stars in cabaret.

Haven Holidays offer self-catering caravans and bungalows in three 'Big all-action Holiday Parks', five 'Family-sized Holiday Parks' and a range of 'Small and friendly Holiday Villages'.

Holimarine feature three Holiday Villages and a range of Caravan Parks, all self-catering.

Hoseasons although not primarily in the holiday centre market feature a number of Holiday Parks, Holiday Villages and Country Clubs in their Holiday Homes brochure. They vary widely in character from high quality country clubs with the emphasis on sports such as golf and tennis, to caravan parks with the minimum of central facilities.

Ladbroke Holidays offer a mixture of chalets, flats, caravans and tents in four Supercentres (for a 'bubbling, action-packed' holiday), three Holiday Centres ('not quite so hectic') and Holiday Villages ('a relaxing atmosphere'). Two centres do offer full- and half-board holidays although most clients self-cater.

Leisure offer 'Luxury' caravans and chalet parks with varying facilities in 15 or so locations, all self-catering.

Pontin's operate nearly 30 Holiday Centres in England, Wales and Jersey mainly offering full board or self-catering holidays. The age at which children are welcome varies from location to location with only a few welcoming babies under 6 months while others stipulate a lower age limit of 2, 3 or 4 years.

Warner offer full-board holidays at seven Holiday Villages and several Club Hotels. Not all of them offer facilities for children.

In addition there are numbers of independently run centres. We have been sent favourable reports of The Savoy Country Club in the Isle of Wight and Gunton Hall Holiday Club, which is associated with, and offers unrestricted access to, Pleasurewood Hills Theme Park at Lowestoft. Each of these has individual characteristics which distinguishes it from the chains. For independent centres *Lets Go To a Holiday Centre* can be obtained free from the National Association of Holiday Centres.

In Ireland the Trabolgan Holiday Centre in County Cork is featured by both B & I Ferry Holidays and by Sealink Holidays. This too features a sub-tropical 'Swimming Paradise'.

Special facilities for children

Entertainment in holiday centres is specifically geared towards 'Happy Families' and the fact that 'Happy kids make a happy holiday'. Wherever organised entertainment is provided it will include something for children . . . all day and every evening too. This varies in style from the legendary Butlin's talent contests to fancy dress parades, discos and video shows, healthy outdoor pursuits like swimming lessons and football coaching. Facilities are generally of a high standard with adventure playgrounds, indoor and outdoor pools and children's clubrooms. At the largest centres like Butlin's there may be as many as 5,000 children in residence in any one week in August so facilities have to be good.

Children's Clubs with specially selected representatives, Redcoats, Bluecoats, Aunties or Uncles are often provided. These help to give a focus to your child's day as well as an element of supervision and guidance for younger ones.

Butlin's operate BATS (Butlin's Active Teens) for 13 to 16 year olds; this offers team competitions following a theme to 'thrill and test' the teenagers. 913 Club entertains 9 to 13 year olds with competitions as well as fun, games and discos. Beaver Club is for 6 to 9 year olds with competitions, sports days, fancy dress, discos, etc.

Haven Holidays provide Havenmates 'to keep everyone happy . . . they organise a full programme of activities – especially in the bigger Parks where there's action-packed entertainment, day and night.'

Ladbroke Holidays have, at nearly every location, a resident children's entertainer and a 'supersonic' Starcruiser Club for 4 to 14 year olds with its own 'space-age' clubroom.

Pontin's enrol all children in their Crocodile Club. Entertainment 'is arranged by a much-loved Pontin's "Auntie" or "Uncle".' There is a large choice of activities from giant inflatables to rambles for smaller children while the older ones can enjoy BMX bikes, video games and the 'chance to body-pop to the disco beat'.

Warner operate the Dodgers Club for 10 to 15 year olds offering 'discos, excursions, sports competitions . . . they can learn new sports, like archery, tennis or BMX biking.' For under 10s you can 'leave your children in the safe hands of . . . "Aunties" and "Uncles"' at the Wagtails club.

If you have a child too young to join one of the activity clubs but too old to come under the care of the nursery with the babies, and of an age when he or she needs your constant attention, you will find that Butlin's, Pontin's and Warner have suitable playrooms where a playgroup is held for pre-school children.

Child listening patrols are operated in a high proportion of centres. When your child is eventually prised away from all the fun and drops into bed exhausted you can, if you have any energy left yourself, return to watch the 'late-nite cabaret', secure in the knowledge that you will be told if they wake in the night screaming.

Going with babies and toddlers

If you have a small child then a holiday centre could offer you the closest thing to a 'real' holiday, but a number of centres do not accept tiny tots, while Pontin's and Warner will only offer you a catered holiday.

There is usually no charge for taking a baby, or for food where applicable, and cots and high chairs are available everywhere, normally at no additional cost for catered visitors. Free nappy washing is offered at Butlin's, Pontin's and Warner. A buggy can sometimes be rented and there is other equipment at a hire shop on-site. There are nurseries and playgroups at the larger centres:

Butlin's have qualified children's nurses operating 'the nursery where they can sleep peacefully or play under the watchful eye of Matron and her staff.' The Night Owl service looks after babies of under 9 months in the nursery in the evening, while older children are looked after by the Child Listening Patrol.

Pontin's offer a Baby World nursery for under 2s at most centres. These are run by qualified nursery staff and offer both childcare and, in some places, a toddlers' dining room.

Warner have a nursery at each centre where you can leave your baby with trained nursery staff.

The cost

A catered holiday at a holiday centre is modestly priced in comparison with family hotels of similar standard. Expect to pay between £120 and £150 per adult per week in high season for full-board. Child discounts vary with the age of the child and season. Free spaces for one child 2 to 9 years sharing with two adults are available throughout the season. Where these are not available discounts of 30% or more are generally on offer at all times for children up to 15 years (Ladbroke, Pontin's and Warner) or 14 years (Butlin's).

Self-catering accommodation is usually priced by the unit so that there are no child discounts. Prices for a six-bed unit in high season range from £130 for a Ladbroke Supertent up to around £400 or more at Butlin's for de luxe accommodation. You will pay £250 to £300 per week for a party of six in a standard chalet in school holidays and around £200 to £250 for four. Butlin's generally costs more than the others, reflecting the better facilities and 24-hour entertainment.

Nearly everything is included in the price you pay so you will not be constantly dipping into your pocket.

Camping and Caravanning

This can be the most basic form of self-catering holiday (depending on your equipment), but as any committed camper or caravanner will know, the joys of being out of doors all day and night should far outweigh the discomforts.

Tents

Before deciding to camp, you should consider your children's reactions to:

- creepy crawlies
- the dark (constant torchlight is not the ideal solution)
- communal showers and smelly toilet blocks.

Solving the problem of how to get the washing dry could be more difficult when camping in a tent than on any other type of holiday. It may be sound advice to go thinking that if the weather is awful you will just pack up and come home.

Even if this sounds rather daunting, camping really is worth it judging by the comments we have received. One moderately enthusiastic before-children-camper tried a week with 3 and 2 year olds in borrowed equipment and now scans the small ads for kit! The same children start asking when they are going camping again as soon as summer comes. After all, a campsite can be very close to the beach and well away from civilisation, yet with other families around. You will pay far less than renting anything else in an equivalent position.

If you do not have equipment and have not tried this type of holiday before, you would be well advised to hire or borrow for your first holiday. Rentatent offer tents for hire from the London area. Check your yellow pages for a convenient, local, tent hire source.

Some site-owners and holiday operators are beginning to hire out ready erected tents in Britain. These have long been available in Europe.

If you want to buy or hire equipment, refer to a specialist book first:

Camping In Comfort, written for families camping both in Britain and Europe, is packed with useful information.

The Spur Book of Family Camping is a glossier, more expensive publication covering much the same information.

You can purchase secondhand equipment easily: frame tent, cooker, table and chairs for £100–£200 as an alternative to upwards of £250 for new and less luxurious equipment. The paraphernalia takes up a lot of boot space so you need a large car, a roof rack or a trailer to hold it all. Try the tent out in your own back garden for a weekend first, so you will learn how to get it up and also acclimatise your children to it. As it may get very cold at night think about taking duvets rather than sleeping bags.

Caravans

These can be hired on sites which may have from 5–300 vans. In a caravan you are better protected from the weather than in a tent and domestic details may be easier.

People we have spoken to extol the joys of early and late season weekends when, for minimal cost, they can explore new areas. Kids also appreciate the existence of their own loo.

Camper vans

These are very similar to caravans, and with one you will have only one vehicle on the road. They are, however, expensive to hire and can have cramped living accommodation. Without an adjustable roof, you have to be under 1.5 m (5 feet) tall to stand up with ease. We know three families who jointly own a camper. They take it in turns to use it and share the cost of maintenance.

Touring sites

When choosing a caravan site or a campsite, decide your preference from the following list:

- size of site (would you prefer it to be tents only?)
- amenities (the number of toilets, showers, etc., compared to its size)
- proximity to the beach and shops (is there a shop on the site?)
- playground
- are dogs banned or do they come and remove the sausages off your barbecue?
- is the site level?

Some sites will offer much more; maybe swimming pools, a bar, a restaurant or a launderette. In general, these will be the larger sites (in excess of 60 pitches for launderettes) or attached to sited caravan parks (for swimming pools).

To find a site for either your tent or caravan look at one of the following directories, but do remember that you will need to book a site in popular spots during the summer school holidays:

AA Camping and Caravanning in Britain lists about 1000 graded, inspected sites which all accept caravans as well as tents.

The Camping and Caravanning Club of Great Britain provides a directory for members although membership is not necessary for use of all the thousands of sites listed in Britain and Ireland. This is the most comprehensive guide and includes small isolated sites with few amenities.

The Caravan Club staffs 180 caravan sites and provides access to 4000 more with five or fewer pitches for members.

Camping Sites in Britain is a *Camping* magazine 'extra'. It lists 1800 sites and is primarily intended for the tent camper in Britain and Ireland. There is no indication of size.

Caravan and Camp Sites in Britain lists 2000 sites ranging from the tiny to very large. It contains no individual site price details.

Good Camps Guide for Britain features about 150 sites personally known and liked by the author.

Practical Camper Sites another magazine's guide, lists 800 sites. The entries are not consistent, presumably because they are written by the owners.

RAC Camping and Caravanning Campsite Guide – GB & Ireland lists their inspected sites.

In addition the regional tourist boards produce lists of camping sites and there are also sites provided by the National Trust and the Forestry Commission.

Ready erected tents

Modernline offer these on one site in Jersey.

Preston Sunroutes feature two sites in Jersey.

Queensway Camping Hire book one site in Sussex.

Rentatent offer one site in Cumbria.

Ladbrokes . . . see Holiday Centres.

Pre-pitched caravans

These are available on huge sites with a multitude of amenities which are included in the Holiday Centres section. There are smaller sites without non-stop entertainment, some of which are available through:

B & I Line who offer 27 sites around the coast of Ireland.

Cade's Self-Catering Holiday Guide primarily features caravan parks of different sizes and amenities.

Hoseasons feature a number of smaller sites in Britain.

The Scottish Tourist Board offer two caravan parks.

Sites that have caravans for hire are indicated in three of the directories: *AA Camping and Caravanning in Britain*, the *Good Camps Guide* and *Practical Camper Sites*.

Some caravan owners hire out their vans: try your local paper's small ads. Question the owner closely about the site, not just about the accommodation.

Camping with children

Some sites have a playground, but where there are other caravans or tents there will always be other children!

You should be aware that your fiddly fingered toddler will find the camping gas cooker tantalising and easily accessible from the open plan living space.

The cost

The cost of using a site is about £3–£7 per night for a tent or caravan with the actual amount depending on facilities, distance from the sea and season.

Hiring a tent and other equipment will cost £80–£120, varying with size, for two weeks in high season.

A ready-erected tent for four in Jersey will cost £500 for two weeks in August.

A sited mobile home will cost £300 for a fortnight in Cumbria or Scotland and £400 in Ireland (including the crossing).

If you take equipment, whether hired, borrowed or your own, to a site, you will need to budget for your travel costs and some sort of fuel (normally camping gaz).

Short Breaks and City Holidays

Secondary holidays, including the weekend break, are one of the fastest growing sectors of the travel market. They are geared as much towards families as to quiet weekends without children.

Whatever the reason for a short break it is possible to secure a bargain whether in a businessman's hotel at the weekend or an empty resort hotel or cottage in the winter months.

A high proportion of people choose a short break in one of Britain's cities. Many families will spend a few days in London to show the children the sights. Others go to historic centres like Bath, Chester, Edinburgh and York. It is certain that these holidays will not be totally ruined by the vagaries of the weather.

The following suggestions form a far from exhaustive list and are intended to offer merely a taster of what is available. Further details of most holidays are given elsewhere in the book.

VISITING LONDON

This is undoubtedly the single most popular destination for a short break.

What to do

There are several useful children's guides to London and its sights.

Capital Guide for Kids provides information on children's theatres, playschemes, etc., as well as the usual, and not so usual, sights.

Children's Guide to London gives 13 walks off the tourist beat which any historically minded 8 year old, or older, will enjoy. Public conveniences and suitable eating places en route are listed.

Children's London a booklet from the London Tourist Board which gives basic information on all the sights of interest.

Discovering London for Children in the delightful 'Discovering' series lists and describes 44 things to do and places to visit including the usual sights and one or two off the beaten track. This book is especially aimed at those between 10 and 16.

Kids' London is a comprehensive guide to all facilities, entertainment and sights for children. Worth buying if you visit often or want to do more unusual things.

When planning your itinerary bear in mind that children get exhausted quickly so do not attempt too much on each visit and don't be disappointed if the highlight of the trip in retrospect was the visit to Hamleys ('the largest toy shop in the world').

Taking a tour

If the whole family is not familiar with London you will find that orienting yourself is essential to make the most of a brief stay. You should start your first holiday, at least, with a sightseeing bus trip: the best value is offered by London Regional Transport's (LRT) one and a half hour Round London Sightseeing Tour which leaves at least hourly until 5 pm all year round from Grosvenor Street (Victoria), Piccadilly Circus and Marble Arch amongst other places. Tickets may be bought on the bus or at a discount from the LRT Travel Information Centres at Piccadilly Circus, Euston, King's Cross, Oxford Circus and St James's Park and at Tourist Information Centres.

How to get around

It is useful to have a copy of the free LRT Official Tourist Information folded map which shows the main tourist attractions, bus stops and tube routes in the centre. Or if you are walking around buy Bartholomew's *Handy Map*, which is more detailed, unfolds easily, is virtually indestructible and shows public loos.

If you are planning to cover several sights in one day you will almost certainly find it worthwhile to get one of the various travel passes available from Travel Information Centres and Underground stations. If you are contemplating a card that covers more than one day, weigh the cost carefully against the number of journeys you are likely to make, bearing in mind that you will run out of steam after a few days.

London Explorer tickets allow unlimited travel on all red buses and tubes, throughout the LRT area, at all times. They can be bought to cover one, three, four or seven days and cost between £3.50 (one day) and £16 (seven days); £1.30 and £4 respectively for children.

Travelcards allow similar travel for one and seven days. The one-day card costs £1.70 (child, 80p), to cover most of London, but travel must start after 9.30 am. The seven day card has unlimited hours, requires a photocard and varies in price according to 'zone' of travel. For example, in the central zone (where most of the sights are to be found), a weekly travel card will cost £4.80. Good value if you are staying in the centre for a few days. Photocards are issued free, but you have to provide a photograph for each member of the family.

One Day Capital Cards allow unlimited off-peak travel by bus, tube and BR in the LRT area. Most valuable if you are planning to stay in Outer London where a BR station is the most convenient starting point, or for the days when you plan to visit sights on the edge of London like Kew Gardens or Greenwich. They cost £2.50 (child, £1.25) for all zones. You can also get a seven day card, which requires a photocard, and for which the price varies according to the zones covered.

Where to stay

Staying with friends or relatives certainly keeps the cost down, although it may cost you more in fares. Virtually all the hotel groups offer London Breaks, with or without rail travel. When you plan where to stay remember that it is hardly worth bringing a car into the central area as parking is scarce and expensive.

However, you do not need to pay hotel prices: the London Convention and Visitor Bureau produces a guide on *Where to stay in London* which covers 400 hotels, guesthouses, bed and breakfasts, and self-catering apartments. For those looking for a budget break there are five Youth Hostels, including centrally situated ones in Earl's Court and Holland Park offering bed and breakfast to members all year round for under £7, £5 for children. A little more luxurious accommodation is offered in university vacations through the British Universities Accommodation Consortium. King's College in Kings Road, Chelsea, King's College in The Strand and Queen Elizabeth College in a charming part of Kensington are all within walking distance of interesting sights and offer bed and breakfast with single rooms for about £10.

HOTEL BREAKS

Any hotel will take a booking for just one night (although hotels in resorts may be unwilling in high season), but if you want to go away for two nights there are more advantageous 'bargain break' deals. You could start by looking at the Herald Holiday Handbook *Mini-Break Holidays in Britain* although it is better to visit your travel agent for brochures.

A number of hotel groups offer special deals with families in mind. The hotels vary from small country inns to concrete and glass structures in London and other city centres. Although the latter may sound less attractive, they are more keen to fill their empty beds at the weekends and thus offer incentives to take the children. The general formula is an 'all-in' deal for two nights dinner, bed and breakfast (bed and breakfast only in London hotels) and you can share your room with as many kids as you can fit in at no charge, although you will generally have to pay for the meals that they eat. If you do not relish the idea of sharing your precious luxury bedroom with the brood, some companies will let under 15s have their own room free of charge (Crest Hotels) or for a flat rate of about £15 for the room (Holiday Inns and Ladbroke Hotels). The hotel chains are falling over themselves to provide enticing incentives to persuade the children to induce you to choose a particular hotel group. Funbags, T shirts, special menus (from Monty Lion's menu at Mount Charlotte Hotels to Hungry Bear and the Munch Bunch at THF) and free entrance tickets to local attractions are liberally promised, not to mention swimming lessons, videos and breakfast parties on Sunday morning to allow you that rare lie in.

TASTER WEEKENDS

Holiday Centres

The prospect of going to a holiday camp may fill you with horror, but out of season they are not quite the same as the clients are there for a restful break. Children will have a wonderful time and even if your preconceptions do all come true you will at least have seen a new part of the country while the children have fun.

Nearly all centres are happy to take bookings for a minimum of either two or three days, varying from company to company. Some restrict holidays to weekly bookings at Easter and in July and August.

Special interest and activity breaks

A list of sources under Activity and Hobby Holidays on page 94 gives some ideas for specialist weekends. The following are just a very small sample:

Birdwatching with Ladbroke Hotels and THF, both in conjunction with the RSPB.

Boating with Blake's, who offer 'Blakeaway' weekends, and Hoseasons. Both allow three-day breaks before mid-May and after mid-September.

Computing with Crest Hotels with courses on programming for both adults and children in four locations.

Cycling with EACH who offer two, three or four nights at a hotel with cycles provided. You can stay in Cambridge or Saxmundham, or tour Suffolk.

Family fitness weekends with Ladbroke Hotels in three locations.

Mystery Weekends, not really aimed at the family but they could be a good choice for over 12s, with Highlife Breaks.

Riding from dozens of independent centres as well as THF hotels.

SuperTed weekends in Llandrindod Wells in either a hotel or guesthouse – definitely for the very young, organised by the Heart of Wales Tourist Association.

Walking can be arranged any weekend from any Youth Hostel, HF centre or CHA centre (Easter to the end of October).

Multi-activity breaks are difficult to find, partly because the summer courses usually utilise boarding schools and are simply not available on the average weekend, and partly because it is difficult enough to grasp one activity in a two-day weekend let alone mastering several. The nearest thing is perhaps Crest Hotels' 'Weekend of a Lifetime'. These are held throughout the year at four hotels; adults are expected to go off sight-seeing while the children enjoy general and special activities. There is a special programme for 3 to 6 year olds so even the little ones can join in. Under 15s get all this for nothing if they are with two adults, and can even have a separate room.

Self-catering weekends

Few owners actually advertise weekend rentals in the out-of-season months; we can only suppose that the amount that people are prepared to pay in the middle of winter will simply not cover the cost of advertising and management. So if you want a property simply ring an agent or owner advertising in the usual places and ask if they are prepared to do a deal. If there is someone on hand to turn on the heating and check it all when you go, they will probably be only too happy to have you. The English/Welsh/Scottish Country Cottages group have over 450 properties designated as suitable for mini-breaks and off-season holidays.

Farm weekends

Anyone advertising in the Farm Holiday directories will be happy to have you to stay for the weekend, particularly outside the summer school holidays.

Self-Catering

Many families will always choose the self-catering option without a second thought. They have the freedom to eat where they want, and do not have to worry so much about noise, manners or their family's strange habits.

The choice of accommodation is enormous – from high rise apartments on the Spanish Costas and holiday villages in Lanzarote to luxury villas with a pool in the Algarve or a modest couple of rooms around a courtyard in Greece; from Scandinavian holiday villages to rural gîtes in France.

The distance of your chosen destination from the channel ports will usually determine how you get there, and this in turn will govern the sources of accommodation, as companies tend to specialise in air holidays or self-drive holidays, but not both. We have, therefore, split this section to clarify the information.

INCLUSIVE SELF-CATERING HOLIDAYS BY AIR

Accommodation

Most families will take an apartment or villa in a complex, generally with some communal facilities such as a swimming pool and gardens. Larger developments may have a supermarket, restaurant, bar, tennis court, entertainment, etc. There are dozens of companies offering such holidays including the major tour operators many of which have a separate self-catering brochure (e.g. Horizon, Thomas Cook, Thomson). You will also find that your travel agent has brochures for large self-catering specialists like OSL.

A significant minority will choose a free-standing villa, or an apartment in a small complex with no communal facilities. These tend to have more character and privacy, are more likely to provide space for two or more families sharing, and with locals for neighbours will probably give you a better flavour of the country you are visiting. This type of accommodation is individually described in the brochures with a description of each unit so that you can easily assess its suitability. The mass market companies do not operate in this way, although your travel agent will have brochures for OSL Villas with Pools, Sunmed and Timsway among others.

For a wider choice you will have to turn to the specialists who usually operate on a direct-sell basis (i.e. are not available through travel agents). These include large, well-established companies like Meon Villas and Travel Club of Upminster. To find such a company offering accommodation in the country that you are planning to visit you should scrutinise the columns of *The Sunday Times* or *The Observer*.

Special facilities for children

An increasing number of companies are making special provisions for children. In 1986 the following operators featured one or more apartment complexes with something special for younger members of the family. Further details of the individual mini-clubs are given in the chapter on Hotels Abroad.

Club Cantabrica have a Kiddies Klub on the Costa Dorada and the Adriatic Coast of Italy, where they run apartment and beach chalet holidays.

Cosmos offer two apartment blocks in Ibiza and Majorca which share an OK Club with a neighbouring hotel so that entertainment is always on tap for 2 to 11 year olds.

Falcon Family Holidays offer apartments on the Costa del Sol, Majorca, Tenerife, Portugal and Malta. All the holidays offered in this sector of the Falcon programme offer mini-clubs geared towards under 12s. Falcon Family Holidays also provide a room patrol service in the evenings, a buggy hire service and communal laundering facilities for mothers.

Global run Wizzy Clubs associated with six apartment complexes in Majorca, Ibiza, Mainland Spain, Gran Canaria, the Algarve and Malta.

Holiday Club International offer a self-catering option at three clubs in Majorca, Sardinia and Yugoslavia. Each of these has a children's entertainment programme as well as the usual sporting facilities which differentiate holiday clubs from hotels.

Horizon Villas and Apartments in seven locations are associated with a Hippo Club. These include complexes in the Algarve, Corfu, Mainland Spain, Ibiza and Minorca. Hippo Clubs are geared towards 3 to 11 year olds.

Lancaster Family First Holidays feature apartment holidays with Children's Clubs, day nurseries and other special services for families with children (buggy hire, laundry rooms, bedtime stories and a nurse on hand).

Sunmed operate the Sunbeam Club in some of their resorts in Greece; in 1986 these were on the islands of Zante, Corfu, Lesbos, Ketalonia and on the mainland at Tolon. They offer free organised fun for 2 to 11 year olds regardless of where they are staying in the resort. Therefore, unlike the other schemes covered here, you may have to take your child into town to join the club if your villa is on the outskirts.

Thomson offer their Big T Club at three apartment and villa complexes in Spain and the Balearics.

Tjaereborg feature three apartment complexes with a Tjaerebear Club for 3 to 10 year olds. These are on Majorca, Lanzarote and Tenerife. In addition they offer holidays at the Club Praia da Ouro Apartments on the Algarve with a full programme for children.

The cost

Self-catering accommodation abroad is usually priced in much the same way as a hotel room, i.e. the price given is inclusive of the air fare, transfer and accommodation. The price charged per head varies with the size of the party, so that a two-bedroomed flat will be quoted perhaps on the basis of three, four or five occupants. The total cost for five people is therefore considerably higher than for three as it includes five air tickets, but the *per capita* cost will be perhaps 20% lower on a fortnight's holiday. Some companies quote a basic *per capita* price and then charge a weekly supplement payable by each client for 'under occupation'.

Children's discounts are not usually quite as favourable for self-catering as for hotel holidays. Some 'free' holidays are available but free children do not count towards the party size (except with Horizon), thus increasing the cost for everyone else. In an extreme case this results in a saving of only a few pounds over the same family claiming that tour operator's normal 50% discount.

In summer 1986 the following were the main companies offering free holidays in apartments and villas: Aegean Turkish, Airtours, Arrowsmith, Blue Sky, Broadway, Cosmos, Ellerman Sunflight, Falcon Family Holidays, Global, Horizon, Intasun, Lancaster, NAT Holidays, Olympic, OSL, Skytours, Sunmed, Thomas Cook and Tjaereborg.

The companies on pages 66–67 have been identified as offering particularly favourable discounts in 1986.

It is difficult to offer a guide price for these holidays as the facilities vary so much. The least a family of four would pay in August for a one-bedroom apartment in Torremolinos with, for example, Horizon would be around £800, but you will have to pay for food on top, giving you a holiday for four for under £900 if you ate in all the time. However, the same family could pay £2000 for a villa with its own pool, just up the road in picturesque Mijas, and still have to buy their food.

Some companies offer optional package deals to include a car (e.g. Meon Villas) while others find that a majority of clients rent a car to meet them at the airport and thus the cost of transfers from the airport is not included in the tour price (e.g. Beach Villas). Car hire can be an expensive extra, and one which you will find it difficult to avoid if you choose an

Self-Catering Holidays by Air: The Best Discounts Summer 1986

The following discounts to a family with two adults and two or more children. If you are travelling with other adults you may find that discounts for second and subsequent children are better than we suggest. Discounts apply to two week holidays.

Company	Discount for first child	Discount for second child	Qualifying ages	Notes
Arrow	5–20% off	5–20% off	2–11	
Arrowsmith	Free or 10–50% off	10–50% off	2–11	
Balkan	40%	Nil	2–12	
Beach Villas	10–50% off	10–50% off	2–11	12–15s quality for £15 reduction in low season.
Blue Sky	Free or 5–35% off	5–35% off	2–11	
Broadway	Free or 20–40% off	10% off	2–10	
Cosmos	Free or 10–70% off	10–70% off	2–11	Selected apartments only.
	10–70% off	10–70% off	12–15	
Ellerman Sunflight	Free or 10–55% off	10–55% off	2–11	
Enterprise	10–40% off	Nil	2–11	One child space available per 2 adults. Teenage discounts on selected holidays only.
	5–20% off	Nil	12–15	
Falcon Family Holidays	20–50% off	Special price of £39	2–16	Special price applies all season with no restrictions.
Falcon	10–40% off	10–40% off	2–11	One child discount per adult.
Global	Free or special price £89 or 15–30% off	15–30% off	2–16	Free holidays throughout the year; special price holidays must be booked by a certain date.

Holiday Club International	Free or 20–40% off	20–40% off	2–11	
Horizon	Free or 15–40% off	Nil if only two adults	2–10	Each child must be accompanied by two fare payers.
Intasun	Free or 10–50% off	10–50% off	2–10 or 16	Child price applies to any number of children sharing with two adults.
Lancaster Family First	Free or 20–35% off	20–35% off	2–12 or 16	Unlimited free holidays for those booking before end of December for selected periods. Age limit varies.
Olympic	Free or 15–50% off	Nil	2–11	Unlimited free holidays for first child outside high season if booked before end of January.
OSL	Free or 5–50% off	5–50% off	2–11	Child price applies to any number of children.
Starvillas	5–25% off	5–25% off	2–16	
Sunmed – Go Greek	Free or up to 20% off	Nil	2–11	Unlimited free holidays, one child per per two adults, all season on holidays booked before mid-January.
Thomas Cook	Free or 15–50%	Up to 50%	2–11	If a free place is taken up no discount for second child.
Thomson Villas and Apartments	15–60%	15–60%	2–11	
Travel Club of Upminster	Nil or 50%	Nil or 50%	2–19	Number of 50% discounts depends on size of villa chosen.

NB: Percentages are approximate where cash discounts are shown by operators.

isolated complex or villa. When you choose your accommodation do check whether a car is necessary and how much it will cost. In high season it is essential to book in advance if you need a car for the whole holiday, and the hire charge is usually lower for a comparable car with similar reliability than for rental on the spot. Out of season you may be able to do a better deal on the spot but you may not think it worth the hassle of spending your first day shopping around for the best bargain.

SELF-CATERING DRIVE YOURSELF HOLIDAYS

This type of holiday can either be arranged independently through an international letting agency or directory, through friends or by renting a property found in a small ad in a newspaper. Alternatively, the ferry operators and a mass of smaller companies organise rental, insurance, maps, overnite stops, route planning and your passage across the channel. Whichever way you book, you are likely to find yourself in a free-standing cottage, gîte or house if you choose Atlantic or inland France (the most popular destination), Denmark or Italy, while if you go to other countries the choice is usually confined to purpose-built holiday villages or blocks of apartments close to the sea where space is at a premium.

Travelling independently will require an element of bravado if you are not accustomed to this type of holiday. Be adventurous! We had reports of people organising their own holidays not just in France but also in Spain, Switzerland and Denmark. As well as small ads, personal contacts and the tourist offices, some of the following agencies may cover your chosen destination. These sources are invariably more economic than going through a tour operator and each of them will make ferry bookings on your behalf if required:

Danish Summerhouses These are privately owned holiday homes available for letting when not in use by the owner. They are individual cottages and houses, usually recently built with modern amenities and good heating and insulation. They tend to be grouped together and may either be near the sea or in the countryside, although the latter are not likely to be more than 30 miles from the coast. Although there is no central list of properties the Danish Tourist Board will provide a list of about 90 booking agents by region. English is so widely spoken in Denmark that a call to the one in the area or town that you wish to visit will reap dividends.

Fédération Nationale des Gîtes Rureaux de France   This organisation grades and supervises around 32,000 gîtes which are privately owned, modest, rural properties. At the local level, they are administered by the *Relais Départemental*. Many Federation members let their gîtes, particularly those close to the sea, to the tour companies for the whole season, so that they are not available for direct rental.

For lists of gîtes you should look at one of the following:

The French Farm and Village Holiday Guide, a directory, available from bookshops, of 1800 or so gîtes. These can be booked through the *Relais Départemental*: a phone call to France will establish immediately if the gîte you want is available.

Gîtes de France Handbook which is sent to those who pay £3 to become members of the *Gîtes de France* organisation, attached to the French Tourist Office in London. This handbook includes 1500 properties which can be booked through the London office. This organisation also produces an inclusive holiday brochure in conjunction with Sally Line and Sealink Holidays which is available from travel agents.

You should be warned that a gîte may be isolated. We had a report of an abandoned holiday in inland Brittany where there was absolutely nothing for a baby and its parents to do. On the other hand another family found local châteaux, market towns, a river with sand and had an excellent holiday. Remember that the French make good use of their rivers and lakes as leisure areas so that proximity to the sea is not essential.

Interhome is an international agency with a computerised listing of 15,000 properties in Austria, France, Germany, Italy, Spain and Switzerland. There is a rather tedious directory for each country briefly describing all the properties on offer. But do not be put off by this; the accommodation varies from apartments to shepherds' huts and you can even rent half a fifteenth century castle. If you are interested in booking one, you or your travel agent should contact their British office.

Touropa   Part of the TUI group which claims to have access to the largest database of hotel and self-catering accommodation in Europe. This is available at the push of a computer terminal button in many travel agents. The properties are mainly apartments on the Mediterranean coast including Cyprus and Israel as well as the more popular spots.

If you prefer to go on a package holiday, leaving someone else to make the arrangements on your behalf, get hold of the brochures of some of the following companies. The large number suggested for France simply reflects its popularity.

Austria: DER, Tourauto.

Belgium: Belgian Travel Service, Olau, Sealink Holidays, Tourauto.

Denmark: Fred Olsen Lines, Hoseasons, Longship Holidays and Scanhomes.

France: Beach Villas, Bowhill Cottages, Brittany Villas, Brittany Ferries, Falcon, French Leave, French Life, French Villa Centre, Hoseasons, Hoverspeed, Just France, Meon Villas, Pleasure Wood, Sally Ferries, Sealink Holidays, Starvillas, Sunvista, Tourauto, VFB, Vacances and Vacances Vertes.

Finland: Longship Holidays.

Germany: DER, Hoseasons, Longship Holidays, Olau, Sealink Holidays and Tourauto.

Holland: Hoseasons, Olau, Sealink Holidays, Townsend Thoresen and Tourauto.

Italy: Bowhill Cottages, Sealink Holidays and Tourauto.

Norway: Fred Olsen Lines, Longship Holidays.

Spain: Hoverspeed, Sealink Holidays and Tourauto.

Sweden: Longship Holidays.

Switzerland: Sealink Holidays.

We had numerous reports from clients of some of the companies mentioned. They liked the security of having an agent to make the arrangements, send them lists of what to take and knowing that when they were there a local English speaking agent was there to help them if anything went wrong, whether a squabble with the owner (who almost certainly does not speak English) or a medical emergency.

The booking service and available information about the properties vary enormously from company to company. At one end of the range companies like VFB not only have staff that clearly know the properties and will advise impartially about their suitability for particular ages but also, instead of filling their brochure with idyllic pictures taken from precisely the right angle, send interior and exterior coloured photos and detailed, room-by-room descriptions for up to six properties in exchange for a refundable cheque for £10. Similarly, if you choose to go independently and decide to use the *French Farm and Village Holiday Guide* you will find that a telephone call to the appropriate regional office in France will put you in contact with someone who knows the properties individually and probably speaks English. At the other end of the spectrum you will find that if you choose one of the ferry companies, booking staff may have no more information than that shown in your brochures. You could, however, benefit from paying less for the travel element of the holiday.

Special facilities for children

If you want special facilities for the children then you may be disappointed if you take a gîte or free-standing Scandinavian Summerhome. The most child-oriented items you are likely to find are a cot, possibly a swing in the garden and farm animals nearby. However, if you choose accommodation in a Holiday Village you will find swimming pools, play equipment and, best of all, other children.

The cost

Like self-catering accommodation in Britain, holiday houses in northern Europe are generally priced on the basis of a weekly rental. Some companies quote the holiday cost on a *per capita* basis to include one ferry ticket per bed space and one car per house. Any child discount quoted simply reflects the reduced cost of their cross-channel passage.

Independently arranged accommodation is usually cheaper. One family reported finding that the apartment taken through a tour company cost them exactly twice the price had they booked direct through Interhome with whom it was registered.

In addition to the rental of the house and ferry ticket you will have to budget for all those other costs faced by Continental motorists including fuel, motorway tolls, motorail (if you choose this option) and car retrieval insurance.

Hotels

For many families it seems easier to stay in a hotel abroad than one in Britain. European attitudes towards children make for a more relaxed holiday. The better weather will mean that children spend less time cooped up indoors and are less frustrated by the inevitable restrictions of staying in a hotel. There is no doubt that European hotels are cheaper for equivalent comfort than those in Britain.

TOURING HOLIDAYS

For a number of families, pre-parenthood holidays meant touring in a car and stopping where the whim took them. For a few this is still their idea of a holiday (and one family we know did it with two children under 2). Outside school holidays it is quite possible to find suitable accommodation without booking, except on the main radial routes within 100 miles (180 kilometres) of the channel ports and in the centres of major tourist cities like Florence.

We had reports of highly successful fly-drive and car holidays in June and September in France, Sicily, Greece and Sardinia. Many others interviewed said that they could not contemplate the risk and uncertainty attached to a trip where you take pot luck at each hotel and especially not with under 5s. One family related the horrors of trying to make a reluctant 20 month old sleep in a single bed in a hotel with no cot available. They now know how little space there is between two adults in a small French double bed!

SINGLE CENTRE HOLIDAYS

Hotel holidays available as a package cover an enormous range of accommodation from *tavernas*, *hostals* and *pensione* offering bed and breakfast only, and where the residents' lounge is a few tables and chairs under the stars, to high-rise palaces with a choice of restaurants. You will know what appeals to you, but if you are looking for somewhere which you can be certain will provide entertainment especially for families you will have to turn to the major package tour operators who take space in large hotels, often with numerous British clients, always in the most popular spots. These are not for people who want to get off the beaten track, but you can compromise to some extent by choosing such a hotel in Corfu or the Algarve and renting a car.

Most families taking an overseas hotel holiday will opt for a package tour, and several million will travel with the Thomson or Intasun groups. The hotels on offer are generally large, a high proportion having over 200 bedrooms. Many feature a children's swimming pool, baby-sitting, early meal times and special entertainment for younger guests. Contributo's either loved or loathed these holidays: 'It was great to be in a place with other English kids, with a playground and playroom and someone else to clear up the mess from painting.' 'We didn't think much of the pursuits arranged for the children.' 'We had all the disadvantages of a holiday in a noisy resort geared to disco-going teenagers in a hotel with built-in, non-stop entertainment. Yuk!'

Such holidays allow you and your children to pursue separate activities for at least part of the day and evening. If your idea of a proper break is to lie in the sun and acquire a tan then this type of holiday will offer you the opportunity, while your older children and teenagaers can go their own way with some element of supervision.

If, however, you feel that Coca Cola and junior discos are not your preferred way of entertaining the 8 to 13s, but you like the idea of separate supervised activities for the young, we suggest that you try a Holiday Club where the emphasis is towards more conventional sports like windsurfing and tennis.

But Costa Touristica egg boxes are not the only type of hotel in Europe which welcomes children. If you expect to entertain your family on holiday by using your own resources then there are thousands of hotels, coastal and inland, to choose from. The problem is simply one of identifying them before you book!

Accommodation

It would be impossible to list all the hotels which have been reported on favourably by contributors. However, most people would agree that there is an element of luck involved and that the same hotels under new management might be far from welcoming.

When selecting a hotel look out for the following:

Hotels close to sandy beaches expect people to bring children and you can be certain that they will be used to families.

Child-oriented facilities (e.g. baby-sitting, playground and early meals), where they are mentioned, automatically mean that families are welcome. Brochures from companies such as Falcon, Thomson, Olympic and Wings (all of which feature numbers of hotels with under 50 bedrooms) state clearly what is available to guests.

Special discounts   Choose a hotel which offers some free child spaces or is designated 'Family Special', even if special discounts are not available in the week you are planning to travel.

If you prefer a smaller hotel you need to be particularly wary of certain pitfalls concerning the facilities on offer. For example, if you are still depending on a pushchair you do not want to find yourself, as did one of our contributors, in a room on the third floor with no lift and nowhere to store the buggy on the ground floor. Every trip out of the hotel had to be preceded by a major expedition down the stairs with armfuls of baby, beach gear and the all-important wheels.

Special facilities for children

There are numerous play-schemes for 3 to 11 year olds, but they are generally only offered in hotels with over 200 rooms. Daytime activities vary with the number of children, their ages and their interests, from handicrafts and nature trails to organised games and picnics. In the evenings there may be videos, junior discos, fancy-dress parties and bedtime stories. After dark the children's representative will organise the baby-listening patrol so that if children wake up they will see a familiar face.

The clubs are generally free, although Tjaereborg and Falcon make a nominal charge, but you will have to pay if you opt for the organised outings (where applicable) and for any food or soft drinks consumed. They will provide a focus for the children's day and ensure that they make friends.

In the summer the clubs are supposed to start operating from the start of the season, which is around Easter, although we have heard of clubs that close down in May and early June due to 'lack of support'. We feel certain that the same does happen to some of those operated in the winter.

Cosmos   Over 20 hotels in Spain, the Balearics, Tenerife, the Greek mainland, Corfu, Rhodes, Tunisia and the Algarve offer an OK Club in the summer for 2 to 11 year olds with a programme of events for six days a week. There is a Kiddy Patrol up to midnight. Do read the brochure descriptions carefully as, rather surprisingly, some of the OK Clubs do not operate during July and August. The OK Club is run at three hotels in the winter in Tenerife and in Torremolinos.

Falcon Family Holidays feature a few hotels in the Balearics in their predominantly self-catering programme. These hotels offer several clubs for which a small charge is made (but your child will have a T-shirt, hat and badge if he or she decides to join the club). Club 10 is for over 3s and is run for at least five days a week, mornings or afternoons; activities include sports, competitions, treasure hunts and games. Trouble Club is for the under 4s: a supervised nursery/playschool is run for at least one hour a day on five days a week. The latter is outside Club 10 hours so there is no chance of getting rid of all your children at once if you have toddlers as well.

Global   A few hotels in Spain and the Balearics feature a Wizzy Club for youngsters from 3 to 12, usually for six days a week, in summer only. These hotels have a Wizzy Patrol up to midnight.

Horizon   Around 20 selected hotels feature a Horizon Hippo Club in summer for children of 3 to 11. These are in Spain, the Balearics, the Greek mainland, Crete and Corfu. The Horizon representative for children is on duty morning and afternoon six days a week. They organise parties, competitions and games, supervise an early evening meal and read bedtime stories. The 'baby patrol' service operates on the basis of a half-hourly visit to each room up until midnight.

Intasun   The Carefree Club for Kids is available in the summer at a wide range of hotels in Spain, the Balearics, the Algarve, the Canaries,

Tunisia, Yugoslavia, Greek mainland, Corfu and Rhodes for 3 to 12 year olds. 'The club is usually available six days a week when the Kiddies' Rep will arrange a daily programme of events – beach games and sports, rambles, swimming galas, fancy dress contests . . . right up to a bedtime story in the lounge most nights.'

Lancaster   All summer the First Mates Club operates in Lancaster's Family First resorts in Spain, the Balearics, the Canaries, the Algarve, Italian Riviera, Tunisia, Morocco and the Greek mainland for children between the ages of 3 to 12. The club is in session six days a week for at least three hours a day, which may be in the day or in the evening. The programme includes beach trips, picnics, treasure hunts, mini-discos and nature walks as well as a story-time session in the evening. The children's representative operates a room patrol service up to midnight on six days a week. For the under 3s a day nursery is operated for two hours a day, four days a week.

Thomson   A wide range of hotels offer a Big T Club where the Thomson Children's Representative arranges 'lots of fun and games' for those between 3 and 11 years. The Club operates at least three hours daily for six days a week with a room patrol service in the evenings. The summer clubs are run in Spain, the Balearics, the Canaries, Malta, the Greek mainland and Corfu. In winter around 20 Big T Clubs continue the entertainment, mainly in Spain and the Balearics but also in Tunisia, Malta and the Canaries.

Tjaereborg   A couple of hotels feature the Tjaerebear Club for 3 to 10 year olds for three hours a day for six days a week. These sometimes mix British and Scandinavian children together (with, no doubt, English as the common language as the Scandinavians start to learn their excellent English as soon as they start school). These appear to offer slightly more constructive activities compared with the other clubs: the children end the week with a cabaret show for the parents so you should get some entertainment out of it too!

In addition to the mini-clubs provided by the tour operators you will notice that the Spanish Sol Hotel Group (not to be confused with Sol Holidays) offer multi-national play-schemes in a selection of their larger hotels. The Sol mini-club provides entertainment for 5 to 11 year olds while the Teenagers Club is run for 12 to 16 year olds at some hotels. The mini-clubs continue throughout the winter in a number of places.

As far as other child-oriented facilities are concerned the major package tour companies invariably give clear descriptions of the services provided, e.g. table tennis, playground and early meals. The sorts of facilities that you can reasonably expect to find are:

A children's pool or a separate area within the main pool cordoned off for safety, which is often featured by medium to gigantic hotels.

Playgrounds which vary from a single swing to a good range of equipment. Beware! It may well not be shaded from the sun and so be unusable in the middle of the day. One mother complained that in Greece her child could not use the metal slide after about 10 am as the heat on his bare legs was agonising. In Spain you may find that the equipment is geared towards tiny tots.

Early suppers are frequently advertised in the brochures. This will not necessarily mean a 5 pm high tea in the dining room, as would be the case in a British hotel offering the same service. In some places it will be an early serving in the dining room of the menu being offered later, while in others a tray will be brought to your room with whatever you wish to order – boiled eggs, glass of milk, etc. Obviously, the service offered will depend on the number of parents wanting to make use of this facility. Be warned, however, that dining room and kitchen staff may not come on post-siesta duty until 6.30 or 7.00 so that the meal could be served quite late by British standards.

Baby listening services are either half-hourly patrols by the play-leader or children's rep in hotels with a mini-club, or by the intercom or phone-off-the-hook method.

Going with babies and toddlers

Most medium and large hotels provide cots (even if this is not clear in the brochures) or will ensure that one is rented for you. In small hotels you should check in advance that one is available. Expect to pay a rental for the cot and linen of up to £2 per night, although a few hotels do offer them free.

Hotels with high chairs are less common, particularly at the small end of the scale, but you will find them in those offering other family-oriented facilities.

Mothers' rooms, with food preparation facilities, laundry equipment, potties and baby baths are found in an increasing number of hotels including those featured by Lancaster Family First, Falcon Family

Hotel Holidays by Air: The Best Discounts Summer 1986

The following table applies to children sharing a room with two adults or in their own room with one other child. Please note that many hotels do not have four-bedded rooms so that there may not be an opportunity for two adults and two children to share. If you are looking for family rooms, Falcon Family Holidays and Lancaster Family First specialise in this type of accommodation. Discounts apply to two week holidays.

Company	Discount for first child sharing	Discount for second child sharing	Discount for children in their own room	Qualifying age
Arrowsmith	Free or 10–50% off	10–50%	Up to 50% per child	2–11
Aspro	Free or up to 25% off	Nil	Nil	2–11
Balkan	40% off	25% off	Nil	2–6
	30% off	25% off	Nil	7–12
Best	10–35% off	Nil	Nil	2–11
Blue Sky	Free or 10–70% off	10–70% off	Nil	2–11
Broadway	Free or 20–40% off	10% off	Nil	2–10
Citalia	35% off all season	35% off all season	10% off per child	2–8
	25% off all season	25% off all season	10% off per child	9–15
Cosmos	Free or 10–70% off	10–70% off	10–50% for first child in Sol Hotels	2–11 or 15
Cricketer Holidays	20% off	20% off	20% off each child	2–18
Enterprise	Free or up to 50% off	Up to 50% off	Nil	2–11
	Up to 20% off	Up to 20% off	Nil	12–15
Falcon	Free or 10–50% off	10–30% off	Nil	2–11
Falcon Family Holidays	Approx. 25% off all season	Special price of £39	Nil	2–11

Horizon	Free or 15–40% off	10–50% off	5–25% for first child	2–10
Intasun	Free or 10–60% off	10–30% off	Nil	2–10, some 11 or 12
Lancaster Family First	Free or special price of £89 or 5–50% off	20–35% off	Nil	2–12, some to 16
Martin Rooks	10–50% off	10–50% off	Nil	2–11
Medallion, Air Malta	10–50% off	10–50% off	Nil	2–11
Medina	Free or 10–50% off	10–25% off	£10 off per child	2–13
Multitours	Free or flat rate (i.e. up to 35% off in high season – no meals)	Sometimes a flat rate (i.e. up to 35% off in high season – no meals)	Nil	2–11
Olympic	Free or 15–50% off	Nil	Nil	2–11
Phoenix	Free 15–50% off	10% off	Nil	2–11, some 2–7
Skytours	Free or 50–75% off, early bookers only	50–75% off, early bookers only	10% off per child	2–11
Sunair	Free or 10–25% off	10–25% off	Nil	2–16
Suntours	Free or 20–40% off all season	Variable	Nil	2–11, some 2–7
Thomson	Free or 15–70% off	15–30% off	10% off	2–11
Thomson Small & Friendly	15–25% off	15–25% off	15–25% off	2–11
Wings	Free or 10–70% off	10–70% off	Nil	2–11
Yugotours	Free or 30–40% off	30–40% off	Nil	2–10

NB: Percentages are approximate where cash discounts are shown by operators.

Holidays, some Sol Hotels and some rather expensive Club Mediterranée hotels. Five Sol hotels feature a 'Family Floor' for those with under 4s where there is a baby minder, playroom, baby shop, etc. If you are particularly concerned about food preparation for your children you would be well advised to select an aparthotel, which is little different from an ordinary hotel except your room will include a kitchenette.

Buggy hire is also available at most of these hotels and a number of others featured by the major tour companies. If you think your child is small enough to be carried (perhaps in a baby carrier) on the journey, or large enough to walk short distances at the airport, then hiring a buggy could cut down the baggage you have to take with you.

The cost

This type of holiday is relatively expensive in comparison to a self-catering holiday, and working out the best financial deal can be a major arithmetical exercise – especially as the hotel of your choice could be featured by five or more different operators. If you want to take two rooms for the family in a large three-star hotel with a mini-club and swimming pools in the school summer holidays you will have no change from £1000 before extras. The twist is that a one star 'character' hotel in the same resort, with inferior facilities by modern standards, will probably cost the same. The tour companies featuring this type of accommodation simply do not have the buying power in terms of numbers of rooms and aircraft seats, nor such low overheads per client as the big operators.

Numerous companies offer free child spaces on hotel holidays outside the school holiday periods and throughout the winter in selected resorts. It is not just the companies with enormous hotels which offer free spaces for children, although you will have a better chance if you choose to go to the mass market resorts. In 1986 the following companies were offering some free holidays for children:

Summer programme   Aegean Turkish, Arrowsmith, Aspro, Broadway. Blue Sky, Cosmos, Enterprise, Falcon, Horizon, Intasun, Lancaster Family First, Lancaster, Multitours, Medina, NAT Holidays, Olympic, Phoenix, Sunair, Suntours, Sunmed, Thomson, Timsway, Wings and Yugotours.

Winter brochures   Blue Sky, Cosmos, Ellerman Sunflight, Enterprise, Global, Horizon, Intasun, Thomas Cook and Wings.

The best discounts that we discovered in 1986 were offered by the companies shown on pages 78–79. Do remember that with different companies offering the same hotel you may be better off with a lower discount with the cheaper company.

Holiday Clubs

The line between holiday clubs and hotel and apartment complexes is ill-defined. For the purposes of this book we include places which call themselves clubs and aim (by definition) to draw you in to meet other families and undertake a multitude of organised activities (usually sporting) to suit your taste and pocket. The club atmosphere is usually engendered by an all-inclusive deal so that, in most, sports facilities, equipment and tuition are 'free', three meals a day are provided and wine is included with meals. There are exceptions, with some clubs following the trend for self-catering while others only provide half-board.

Holiday clubs range in style from the sophisticated and, according to some, pretentious Club Méditerranée to the Holiday Club International, which is closer to Pontin's in terms of the entertainment provided. The latter will certainly suit the taste of many children but if your teenagers are longing to master a watersport then Mark Warner clubs or Club Med will certainly satisfy them.

One of the distinctive features of holiday clubs is that they are international in flavour and give you plenty of opportunity to mix with other nationalities. If you do not find this appealing then you should choose Club Mark Warner, which is exclusively British, or Holiday Club International. If you are keen for you or your children to practise French or German then Club Med or Robinson Club will provide the opportunity. However, you will find English widely spoken by instructors and other staff as well as by a fair proportion of guests.

Do *not* choose a holiday club if you want to absorb the atmosphere of the country you are visiting. They are often well outside the main villages and towns, and most clubs aim to provide sufficient eating, drinking and entertainment facilities to keep you and your money (or strings of currency beads) inside the four walls all day and night. To be fair, the smaller the club, the less likely this is to be true.

Accommodation and special facilities for children

Most of the Holiday Clubs are one of a chain. The following are offered by British tour operators:

Center Parcs in Holland are featured by Sealink Holidays and come with names which are so typical of a Briton's conception of Holland: De Kempervennen, Het Vennenbos, De Eemhof and De Lommerbergen. The centres are complexes of bungalows in forest settings, each sleeping between two and eight. The centre-piece of each one is a covered swimming pool with wonderful facilities for children of all ages and kept, all year round, at 28°C (82°F). As well as slides, waves and jet streams there is a paddling pool and toy animals for toddlers. Outdoor facilities include tennis courts, cycle hire, sailing, fishing, windsurfing and running tracks. Three to 10 year olds are welcome at the kindergartens and there is a baby listening service.

The Parcs are all self-catering but there is a good choice of restaurants on site. For one family with children differing in age from 2 to 10 years the holiday was so successful that they went straight home and booked a repeat holiday, in a different centre, for the following year: 'We wanted a foreign holiday without the hassle of travelling long distances, nor the problems of sunburn, but with a beach for the baby and activites for the older two. We couldn't better a Center Parc with its indoor version of the seaside.'

Club Med has around 50 grass-hutted bungalow and hotel clubs all over the world, of which about half (including both European and distinctly exotic destinations like the Turks and Caicos islands) can be reached by package tour from London. These are definitely at the sophisticated end of the market, with prices to match. Facilities for children of 4 and over are excellent and are run all day every day until 9 pm. About half the resorts have a Kids' Club for over 8s (French school holidays only) and the Mini-Club for 4 to 8 year olds. Small children are only catered for at about eight centres, all of which have a P'tit Club for the 2 to 4 year olds and some of which have a Baby Club for infants from 4 months. There is an enormous range of activities from watersports to golf, from arts and crafts to computer workshops. In the school holidays there is excellent instruction for children all included in the price. 'A really relaxing holiday on which I was able to forget about the baby for hours on end, and to succumb to the pampering while the activities were great for a less lethargic husband,' said one mother. 'But it was definitely important to have a reasonable knowledge of French,' said another.

Club Peter Stuyvesant was started in 1985 and if you can come to terms with the juxtaposition of the name of a tobacco company and a healthy, outdoor holiday you will find an operation not unlike the Mark Warner clubs. They are aiming at the watersports enthusiast so if your family are keen this could appeal. The three clubs are in Malta, Levkas (Greece) and on the Bodrum Peninsula in Turkey. Although there are no special facilities for children, nor a care scheme for the little ones, their attractive child discounts for 2 to 11 years old (50% off in April, May and October) suggest that they are welcome.

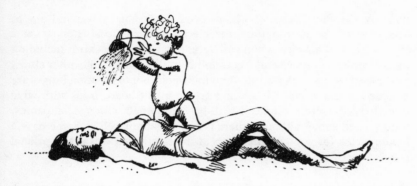

Holiday Club International, now offered as part of the Horizon programme, welcomes children at about 10 clubs in Tenerife and on the Mediterranean in the popular spots of Morocco, the Costa del Sol, the Balearics, Sardinia, Italy, Yugoslavia and mainland Greece. You may self-cater, go half-board or full-board although not all options are available at all clubs. Each offers a children's programme organised by the resident Auntie. This includes competitions, fancy-dress parties and mini-discos. There are day nurseries for smaller children. The clubs will appeal to those who want a holiday where everyone joins in; as in most beachside clubs, a good range of free watersports is available but there is rather more emphasis on the discos, cabaret, darts and poolside sunbathing. The reports of successful holidays at these clubs were spoiled by complaints about the lack of a baby-listening service (in all fairness not advertised in the brochure) so that those with younger children could not confidently leave them in the evenings.

Mark Warner operate six informal clubs of which four welcome children. These are in Skiathos (Greece), Bodrum in Turkey and two in Corsica (one conveniently near the airport at Ajaccio). The clubs are small, with only 50 to 80 guests, and offer a wide range of watersports, including tuition where appropriate, as well as land-based activities like tennis. Trained staff are available to supervise children's activities for 4 to 9 year olds six days a week in the period from mid-July to the end of September. Older children can, of course, participate in water sports and take the opportunity to learn one or more new skills. The house party style means that you have to make a special effort to get time to yourself. One comment from someone who had been to two clubs in consecutive years was that 'it was so intimate that the success of the holiday depended on who the other guests were in the same week.'

Phoenix Holiday Clubs, of which seven are in Yugoslavia and one in Romania, all in unpronounceable places, offer a 'total' holiday at a modest price. This means you will have to pay for a few extras including windsurfing, sailing, rowing boats and baby-listening. Like other clubs, land-based sports such as tennis and mini-golf (not to mention bingo) are included in the price. All holidays are on a half-board basis with wine provided with meals. Children will be entertained with special games, contests and shows although there is no formal mini-club. Some have a kindergarten for younger members of the family but this is an optional extra.

Robinson Clubs in Greece are the German version of the famous Club Med but without the grass huts. They are run on broadly the same lines with less emphasis on watersports and more on the arts – you can try silk screen printing or attend dancing school. Standards of accommodation and food are high and they emphasise that you will be staying in modern comfort, unlike their namesake Robinson Crusoe. There are programmes for children of 4 to 6 years, 7 to 11 years and 12 to 17 years. The five clubs on Corfu, Crete, the Peloponese and on Kassandra in the north are available through Olympic Holidays. There is little point of going to a Robinson Club if Germans, en masse, irritate you with their love of organisation and very different sense of humour. And, as with Club Med, if your family do not speak the language of the majority of guests you may feel very isolated.

As well as the chains of holiday clubs there are independent clubs available through one or more operators. If you are interested in this sort of holiday look for the following which all offer the same formula of sport, sun, entertainment and lots to occupy the children:

Club La Mola on Formentera, operated by Iberotels, which is offered in both the Intasun and Wings brochures.

Club Poseidon on the Gulf of Corinth offered by Intasun.

Cosmos Club Hotel in the Peloponese offered by Olympic.

Forte Hotel Village in Sardinia offered by Citalia is at the luxury end of the scale.

The cost

As the style of the holiday clubs varies widely so do the prices charged. You must expect to pay a little more than you would for a hotel of equivalent comfort. This, of course, balances the amount you would otherwise spend on entertainment and watersports, not to mention wine with your meals. However, you will reap the benefits when it comes to the amount of pocket money required if your family is sports minded; and avoid having someone sidling up to you with the words 'Dad, you couldn't spare another 2000 drachma, could you. . . ?'

Child discounts are variable and can differ from one club to another within a single company. As the prices include more than that in a normal hotel, child discounts are applicable to children not sharing with their parents at Mark Warner, Club Med and Holiday Club International. At the two cheaper chains discounts as high as 20% are available in high season.

Free holidays are not common. In 1986 only Holiday Club International were offering these and then only very early and very late in the season.

A holiday in August for a family of two adults and two children in a separate room would cost around £1200 at Holiday Club International and Phoenix, £2000 at Mark Warner, Peter Stuyvesant and Robinson, and over £3000 at Club Meds in Europe – much more if you want to go further afield.

Camping and Caravanning

If you have never camped abroad and you envisage a holiday with dubious loos, cold water taps dotted here and there and crawling into bed at sunset as your torch is not strong enough to read by, then think again. Continental camp sites can be very luxurious, providing you with comfort only one step removed from a holiday cottage, often with swimming pools, launderettes, restaurants and boating lakes.

But there are drawbacks to these luxury camp sites as pitches are marked out and tents will be close together, giving little privacy. The outdoor sounds of the cuckoos and the grasshoppers may well be drowned by the strains of 'Radio Europe' from the next tent. The disadvantages may be more than compensated for by the freedom of having a self-catering holiday with a campers' restaurant just across the field so that you can hop out, with or without the children, for a ready-cooked meal.

You do not have to own or borrow camping equipment and you need not face the problems of having to select and book a site from a directory. Nor will you have to contemplate pitching a complex mass of canvas and guy ropes in the half light with a brood of tired and fractious children providing not very useful instructions from the sidelines.

You can opt for an inclusive package holiday allowing you the freedom to move from one pre-booked ready pitched tent to another. Or you can rent a caravan on a fixed site and either stay there for the entire holiday or move on after a few days to another van on another site.

TOURING WITH YOUR OWN EQUIPMENT

Many families do have their own equipment or touring caravan and prefer the freedom to wander from site to site as the whim takes them. Although in June and September this is perfectly feasible it may be more difficult in school holidays as sites fill up quickly and tourers may well have to find a space on a site before 3 pm. In popular tourist areas and close to the beach sites are booked up months in advance during school holidays, so make a booking using one of the several good guides without which no camper should venture out of doors. These are:

AA Camping and Caravanning in Europe which covers 4000 sites in 19 countries. Has helpful site booking letters in five languages.

RAC Camping & Caravanning Camp Site Guide – Europe produced in association with the Camping and Caravan Club of Great Britain and covering 2500 sites throughout Europe. It includes personal recommendations from members of the two organisations.

If you would like a do-it-yourself camping holiday but have no equipment, the AA offer a six-person tent with furniture, kitchen equipment and lighting, together with a roof-rack and cover, for around £110 to £135 for a fortnight depending on season and whether you have AA membership. This has to be collected from Dover. They also have four-berth trailer tents and luggage trailers for hire.

In major British cities there are agents who rent out camper vans or Dormobiles which are easier to set up each time you stop but not as comfortable as a touring caravan. These are, however, very expensive.

INCLUSIVE CAMPING HOLIDAYS

Inclusive camping holidays under canvas are a good value alternative to the self-catering flat if you want a seaside holiday with an outdoor feel. 'We had no worries about spoiling the furniture, wasting hotel food or our children being as lonely as they might have been in a cottage in the country.' Unlike a self-catering holiday you are flexible and can take in several areas by moving from camp site to camp site (with a specified minimum amount of time at each), but with small children it may not be worth the trouble of packing twice to move to another site.

We had enthusiastic reports about these holidays and much praise for the operators. 'We would go back with Eurocamp anytime.' 'The Magpie Club (Sunsites) exceeded our expectations' and 'Canvas Holidays really organised the whole thing fantastically' were typical comments. No one could fault the equipment or the enthusiastic young British couriers.

Accommodation

You do not have the expense of buying equipment as you go to a site where the tents are pitched and waiting. Each company varies slightly in what is offered, but it is likely to be fairly comfortable. You will have a frame tent with separate zipped compartments for bedrooms with camp-beds. There will be a fully equipped cooking area usually with the option of a 'fridge. Some companies allow you to opt for your own loo (to save night-time journeys across the field) or even 'cabinettes' which add a proper kitchen and shower room on to your tent. Caravans will have all facilities within them.

Sites have electric points to provide lighting and you will have access to hot showers and normal loos. A number of sites have a launderette, ironing facilities and a games room. If you are away from the coast there could well be a swimming pool and many have other sports and leisure facilities.

Most companies allow self-drive campers to take a holiday of any length over four days starting on any day of the week. The inclusive package will include the ferry ticket for the car and passengers and, if you wish, a hotel or camp site for an overnight stop on the journey to and from your site.

France is the major destination for most families, but there are sites in virtually every European country within driving distance, from Norway to Yugoslavia.

The largest of the many self-drive companies are:

Canvas Holidays with around 90 sites in Austria, Corsica, France, Italy, Switzerland and Yugoslavia.

Eurocamp with nearly 100 sites in Austria, Belgium, France, Germany, Italy, Spain and Switzerland.

Inn-Tent through W H Smith Travel offer around 40 sites in the same countries as Eurocamp.

Keycamp with nearly 30 sites in France, Holland, Italy and Spain.

Sunsites have some 70 sites in Austria, Belgium, France, Germany, Guernsey, Denmark, Italy, Norway, Spain, Sweden, Switzerland and Yugoslavia.

You do not have to travel by car as a number of companies offer excellent value holidays by coach; these tend to be to camp sites and caravan parks beside the Mediterranean and you will not normally have the option of moving from site to site. Companies offering coach holidays include:

Club Cantabrica, to seven resorts in Spain, Italy and France.

Intasun Camping, to seven resorts in Spain, France, Italy and Yugoslavia.

Keycamp offer the option of travelling by coach to six camps in southern France, Holland and Spain.

NAT Holidays take campers to around 20 sites in France, Spain, Italy and Yugoslavia.

Seasons Holidays (Eurocamp's sister company) to 10 sites in the south of France, Britanny, Italy and the Costa Brava.

Tentrek offer eight sites in France, Spain, Italy and Yugoslavia.

Some companies offer the option of flying to your resort, which might be preferable for those with small children. There is also a very small range of air holidays to the Algarve and Greece (Club Cantabrica, NAT Holidays and Tentrek).

Special facilities for children

Camping holidays are the epitome of a family holiday and your children will have a great time with the other children on the site. Many camp sites have play areas, table tennis, mini golf, tennis courts, volley ball, fishing, boating, riding not to mention a swimming pool or nearby beach. Canvas Holidays even offer their beginners' tents at £1 per night so your child or, at a pinch, two children could be completely independent at night.

If your family is keen on sporting activities you could try Eurocamp's category of sites called Sportscamps. These have additional facilities from golf to windsurfing. Competitions are organised during high season for footballers, BMX riders, tennis players, etc. For junior sports enthusiasts, Sunsites organise a summer-long 'Superstars' contest (on the lines of the television programme). Canvas Holidays feature special facilities for water sports enthusiasts: windsurfers, canoes and sailing dinghies are provided free at specified sites, while a small number offer free instruction for beginners by a Watersports Courier. Meanwhile, Keycamp clients have free access to a 'Keycamp Leisure Chest' which is filled with bats and balls, as well as boules for those wanting to try the local sport.

A number of companies offer a more formal play scheme and children's club. You might look for the following when planning a holiday of this type:

Canvas Holidays operate the Hoopi Club for under 14s, which means youngsters are given an information pack and have a weekly get-together at every one of their 90-odd sites. There are also children's couriers at selected locations who organise special programmes every day of the week.

Club Cantabrica offers a Kiddies Klub at three camp sites; the Klub

Hostess is on hand six days a week to take on all-comers between the ages of 3 and 12 for treasure hunts, games, competitions and a children's barbecue.

Eurocamp has 18,000 members in its Junior Eurocampers' Club which is open to all campers between 7 and 13 years. This involves the children all the year round with newsletters, birthday cards and pen pal schemes as well as providing travel packs for their journey. There are special Children's Couriers on about 30 sites who daily organise games and activities for children of all ages.

Inn-Tent shares facilities with Eurocamp and young clients are enrolled in the Inn-Tent Junior Club.

Intasun Camping operate their Carefree Club for Kids, which is aimed at the 3 to 12s, at two sites. The Kiddies Rep arranges a daily programme of 'fun events'.

Keycamp offer a Children's Courier or Children's Club at selected camp sites with the service varying from site to site.

Sunsites enrol all children between 3 and 13 in the Magpie Club, which has a newsletter with competitions and puzzles and issues a highly praised Club Funpack for the journey with colouring, I-spy and stickers to swap with other children. They have Children's Couriers at about 20 sites who arrange activities for younger children in and around the special play tent.

Going with babies and toddlers

If you are travelling with very small children you will find that cots are generally provided free of charge by the self-drive companies. Check beforehand on availablity as some sites do not have cots, notably those in the Intasun brochure.

A baby-sitting service is usually offered by the couriers at an extra charge. If you are concerned about your baby or toddler getting into the cooking area look for a company with a tent design which separates the cooking and living areas, e.g. the Sunsites tents.

The cost

A fixed site camping holiday is not likely to be much cheaper than a self-catering house, villa or flat sleeping six. But you would never be so close to the beach, lake or river bank or have a swimming pool and play equipment in the garden for the same amount of money. For those thinking of taking a caravan the cost will be more.

Self-drive holidays are priced to include the site charge, hire of the equipment or caravan and the cost of the ferry crossing for a car and two adults. A supplement is then charged for each child, depending on age and season, to cover the ferry fare – it may be nothing for under 10s. Thus in August a family of four can expect to pay a basic price of about £500 for a tent sleeping six, with a supplement for each additional adult or child over 13. Some companies do not charge for under 14s while others only allow them to go free outside high season. If you want a caravan, expect to pay £200 extra at peak times.

Coach and air holidays are shown with a price per person. Free holidays, therefore, represent a free place on the coach or aeroplane. These are offered by Intasun and NAT Holidays.

Weekend Breaks

If you cannot go abroad for your main holiday or you just want a taste of another country then the packaged weekend breaks may be for you. However, do not expect a bargain if you choose a city holiday or fly. The only way that you will get a cheap deal is by using up the spare capacity on ferries out-of-season or by staying in businessmen's hotels at a weekend. A combination of the two is the best value for money.

Ferry breaks

For most families, a short break abroad is a quick trip across the English Channel. Bargains can be had in winter when the ferry companies virtually throw the travel element in free. And if you take the car you can load it up with edible and drinkable souvenirs. You can give the children a quick introduction to 'abroad' at a fraction of the cost of a summer holiday, and, if you choose France, a fleeting chance to practise their French.

Ferry breaks are also offered to Holland, Belgium, Denmark and even Spain. However, the further afield you go, be it Brittany or Denmark, the more of your weekend you spend on the ferry. The operators like it because you spend money, but you should consider whether this is your idea of a break.

Ferry breaks are normally offered from the end of September to the end of April although there are variations:

Brittany Ferries offer short breaks with or without a car. You can go to Brittany, Paris (via Caen) and to Spain for just one day, with two days of cruising.

Hoverspeed's *Le Weekend* short motoring breaks brochure offers many different types of hotel within reach of Calais and Boulogne.

Sealink's *Mini Breaks* brochure offers two to four night hotel breaks to France, Belgium, Holland and Germany. You can also choose to go all year round to a Center Parc in Holland for three or four nights.

Townsend Thoresen offer Continental Weekenders at hotels in a ring from Cherbourg in the south to Amsterdam in the north.

Children under 4 are usually free and from 4 to 14 are charged up to £30 for three nights.

Air travel breaks

Air weekends to major cities like Paris, Amsterdam and Bruges tend to be rather higher up the price scale and you could have a week in Britain for the cost of a weekend in Paris. Have a look at National Holidays, Thomson, Paris Travel Service or Time Off if you want a holiday like this, but as child discounts are very limited, they are not really recommended for young children who will not appreciate the finer points of the culture and architecture.

Once children have outgrown unadulterated beach holidays, and if the style of a holiday centre or a holiday club with their wide range of activities and entertainment does not appeal to you, but you would still like an active holiday, the broad category of Special Interest Holidays may be the answer.

There are hundreds of different subjects to choose from, some are highly specialist while others are just relaxed holidays with a theme. The more relaxed it is, the more likely it is to be suitable for children. We have, therefore, excluded the options involving staying in a hotel as on this type of holiday children are usually accepted only on sufferance.

Most of the ideas are British Isles based, as holidays with a theme take your mind off the weather and ensure that even if you encounter a whole week of torrential rain you will have something to show for your efforts at the end of it. A few overseas options are included for those who want both a full-time occupation and a chance of sunshine.

Activity and Hobby Holidays

On these holidays you learn, or improve on, one or more skills in an easy-going atmosphere. You may wonder at the end whether it was really a holiday, given the distance you have run round a tennis court or the energy you have expended on kite-flying! Just bear in mind that a change can be even better than a rest.

Most familiy activity holidays are operated only in school holidays and make use of fairly spartan accommodation in boarding schools, university halls of residence or hostels. The food provided will not be *haute cuisine*, nor usually waitress served.

You can select either a multi-activity package or a single activity centre. There are, obviously, only a limited number of activities where the whole family can join in together on an equal footing.

This book cannot attempt to cover all the options so we suggest you refer to the following for ideas:

Activity & Hobby Holidays, England lists hundreds of centres offering residential courses, usually indicating at what age children are welcomed.

Activity Holidays in Britain & the Channel Islands is full of classified advertisements for accommodation, courses and activities as well as display ads. It features far fewer holidays than the above publication but covers a wider geographic area.

Adventure Holidays by Simon Calder gives a classified list of centres offering particular types of holidays. Although many are for over 16s only, you will find that most have a minimum age shown against the entry.

Discover Young Ireland available free from the Irish Tourist Board.

HF Holidays publish a brochure *Hobby and Special Interest Holidays*. This covers both Great Britain and the rest of Europe.

PGL Family Adventure brochure, covers the British Isles and Europe.

Scottish Youth Hostels action and adventure programmes includes some holidays suitable for families with children.

YHA *Adventure Holidays* programme from their national office covers hostel-based holidays at home and abroad, with a minimumn age of 10 years.

You could also look at the advertisements under the Activity Holidays classification in *The Sunday Times* and *The Observer*.

MULTI-ACTIVITY HOLIDAYS

Most families going together on an instructed holiday will choose this type as individuals can select activities according to their age and interest. You can often spend as many days as you like on one topic and choose half-days for others to fill up the week, perhaps tackling ten or so pastimes during your holiday. You should choose somewhere with subjects sufficiently varied to engender enthusiasm in even the most difficult-to-please member of the family. Do not choose a sports package if one of you yearns to go sketching or learn porcelain painting. Programmes are usually large enough for a parent to slip out unnoticed for sightseeing, shopping or walking trips.

The children will meet many others of their own age, and in a lot of centres will sleep in supervised dormitories while parents are in the less spartan sixth form accommodation. If you choose a course in a university residence it will probably mean staying in adjacent single rooms. Should you want more comfort or to self-cater then look carefully through the brochures.

Here are three centres which either offer a wide choice of activities or welcome all members of the family regardless of age.

Millfield Village of Education at Millfield School in Somerset offers 360 separate courses covering 90 activities from ballooning to spinning. There is a special multi-activity programme for 5 to 13 year olds as well as some courses specially aimed at grandparents. Children can join specialist courses from the age of 8 (5 years for swimming). As well as a junior multi-activity programme there is a crèche for 3 to 5 year olds which is free to residents. In the evening there is an enormous leisure programme with the Village Club (for adults), Club 13 (for over 12s), Pre-teen Club (for 8 to 12s) and Junior Club (for under 8s). Each of you will be charged from £140 for five days, and more if certain courses are selected like hot air ballooning (which costs £60 extra).

PGL Family Adventure offer multi-activity holidays at a number of centres including several near the sea, one in Guernsey and one in Austria. Emphasis is on family activities, especially land and water sports, so do not expect esoteric arts and crafts. There are playschemes at four centres for 4 to 6 year olds and special activities at one centre in Denbigh for 7 to 9 year olds. You can elect to self-cater or take your own touring caravan – preferable perhaps for those with a non-participating member of the family or those with special diets. A full-board holiday in school accommodation costs around £160 per head per week for multi-activities, dropping to £100 or so for non-participating adults and children on the playscheme.

Summer University, held at Loughborough for three weeks each summer, offers 70 different courses for adults. There are special Horizon courses for 13 to 17 year olds and a very active Youth Group for 5 to 12 year olds. Unlike most centres, there are facilities for the very young, as babies under 18 months can be left in the University crèche while a playgroup is organised for toddlers. A week of adult instruction with full board costs from £160 to £210 depending on the subject, Horizon costs £135, Youth Group £110, Playgroup £40, and the babies go free.

SPECIAL INTEREST HOLIDAYS

We have picked out five representative subjects which might appeal to families.

Birdwatching

Quite an array of organisations offer wildlife holidays, the largest organisation being the Field Studies Council who offer some special family courses. In addition, the RSPB offers family birdwatching breaks in conjunction with Ladbroke Hotels, while HF Holidays run one week holidays from six British centres and one in Majorca. All you will need are nature-loving children who can sit still for more than just a minute or two and some old, neutral coloured, clothes. Some of the courses are specifically aimed at beginners, so do not be put off if you think that everyone will be terribly knowledgeable. The cost will depend on the accommodation and starts from about £85 per head for an RSPB/Ladbroke holiday.

Cycling holidays

You can organise this sort of holiday yourself by taking your bikes on the train to your starting point and then cycling between camp sites, youth hostels or B & Bs. However, unless you are very enthusiastic cyclists each member of the family will not own a modern, lightweight, three or more speed bike. And you may prefer the idea of going with a guide, to pre-booked accommodation or in a group. If you go with a specialist company you can always hire suitable touring bikes with panniers, or luggage may even be carried by van between stopping points. Also if you go with a group there will be others around to help when your bicycle gets a puncture or the chain falls off.

But will the children like it? Once a child can confidently ride a two-wheeler and can cope with gears – about 8 years – they will be happy cycling. Ensure before you book that the organiser has the right size of cycle. Pre-school children, large enough to be independent of baby-gear but small enough to sit in a child seat, can be taken along too, with varying degrees of success. Susi Madron writes that 'our daughter, Claire, sat in the child seat for 250 miles through Normandy when she was 5. She did grumble a lot, and we seemed to have to walk up a lot of hills to begin with, but it was still a wonderful holiday for all of us.'

The distance you can expect to ride will depend on the size and stamina of your child and the terrain, but a target of around 30 miles maximum per day is sensible, with if possible a rest day in the middle of the holiday. The notes on the following holidays may give you some ideas:

EACH Cycling Holidays offer British holidays in the West Country, Scotland and East Anglia, with a variety of tours in each area lasting between eight and 15 days. You will cycle with only your own family for company, but you have the back-up of a breakdown service. At a vast cost luggage can be carried from one night stop to the next. If you think that Britain has too many hills, they offer four tours in Holland and four in Denmark with the option of hotels or Youth Hostels. Prices for eight days range from £115 per head for b & b and cycling equipment in Britain, to around £340 per head for half-board in hotels and cycle hire in Denmark.

PGL Family Holidays offer week-long holidays with daily cycle trips from a hotel in the West Frisian countryside of Holland for those with children over 10. The cost is around £170 per head with £10 off for under 18s.

Susi Madron's Cycling for Softies offer touring holidays in five regions of France based on hotels. You could take the tour classified as the 'Gentle Tourer' for seven, nine or 14 days, which changes hotels every other night, or if you are keen go for a 'Whizz' (almost every night in a different place) or an 'Adventurer' where you go off the beaten track and find your own accommodation for 11 out of 14 nights. The cost varies with your destination and your mode of travel to the starting point. As a guide, seven nights in southern Normandy will cost about £245 per head in high season with £13 off for under 14s, while the same holiday in Provence costs £330 with £50 off for under 12s

Triskell Cycle Tours offer a variety of tours in Brittany staying in accommodation ranging from Youth Hostels to hotels. They provide bikes for children from 8 upwards and encourage you to take small children and babies. They have child seats for those up to 40 lb (18 kg) and a trailer to hitch to your bike which contains a carrycot for babies too small to sit on a seat. A seven-day holiday with half-board, ferry fare and cycle is around £150 in hostels for adults, £35 less for under 14s, rising to around £170 for hotels.

Horse-drawn caravanning

All you need for this, the epitome of a slow relaxed holiday, is a love of nature and your friendly four-legged companion (who knows much more about this type of caravanning than you do). Tuition will be given to you on how to harness, handle and drive, so between you and the horse you should get a good chance to explore the byways at a rate of eight or nine miles a day.

CIE Tours offer caravanning in County Wicklow. This is an ideal area for caravanning with contrasting landscapes, quiet roads and lovely beaches. The holiday price includes air or ferry travel from Britain to Dublin and transfers; if you take your own car from England or Wales in August the cost will be around £130 per head with an additional week's rental being in the region of £200 in total.

TAG Adventure Holidays rent out caravans in Powys on the border of England and Wales at around £230 for the whole family, without travel, for a week in high season.

Pony trekking holidays

This is a perennially popular holiday for both children on their own and the whole family. The absolute minimum age is 6 years, although some centres suggest 8 or 9 years and we are inclined to agree. Unaccompanied children have to be older.

You will not need to be a proficient rider to go trekking as your steed will be well used to beginners. You must weigh less than 12.5 stone (80 kg) and have stamina, as in addition to trekking all day you have to look after your mount.

When you select a centre:

● Check that it is a centre with British Horse Society or Ponies of Britain approval as these organisations set guidelines for safety and equipment.

● Check that they take novices if any of you are inexperienced.

● Check that they will lend or hire out safety hats to riders, if you do not own one. Otherswise you must beg, borrow or steal one before your holiday.

There are masses of centres to choose from listed in the guides, in leaflets from the British Horse Society (*Where to Ride* at £1.95 or *Pony Trekking* at 50p) and in *Wales Pony Trekking and Riding*, free from the Wales Tourist Board. If only some members of the family want to ride you might consider either one of the multi-activity centres with a full week riding option (e.g. Millfield Village of Education) or choose one of the Pontin's Holiday Centres with a riding course (four centres). HF offer family riding holidays at two centres where some members of the family could walk or ramble while others go trekking.

A week of trekking will cost around £140 per head with a double room. Children sleeping in dormitories are usually charged less.

Water sports

There are numerous centres offering sailing, windsurfing, water skiing, canoeing and cruising on the lakes and coasts of Britain. Some have special family courses, either involving teaching everyone to handle a sailing cruiser or allowing each person to pursue a different interest.

These holidays are generally for children over 10 years who can swim at least 50 metres. The success of the holiday will, to some extent, depend on the weather. Do check that wet suits are provided in your child's size.

As well as the numerous sailing schools (the Royal Yachting Association has a list of recognised establishments) and water sports centres, you could look at the three HF centres with a course.

If you would rather learn to sail in the Mediterranean look at PGL Holidays on the Languedoc coast of France. These camping holidays offer sailing tuition for those over 6 years; younger children can be cared for by a Beach Nanny so the whole family is welcome. Falcon Sailing welcome older children on all their dinghy and sail-boarding holidays but particularly those in Levkas, Greece, where the winds are lightest. Here they have two members of staff specially to look after 5 to 13s during school holidays. Three youngsters we know had a ball mucking about in boats and learning a bit about sailing as well. If you want a less specialised holiday, several other companies offer free sail-boarding, e.g. Sunmed (self-catering holidays), Mark Warner (Holiday Clubs) and Canvas Holidays (Camping).

Should you want to canoe, PGL will take families with over 6s canoeing on the River Ardèche to visit the famous gorges. You can combine this holiday with dinghy sailing.

It is impossible to give a guide price for these holidays as the variation in accommodation, travel expenses, equipment and tuition is exceptionally wide.

Holidays Afloat

Boating can provide a tremendous holiday for children old enough to adhere to the necessary safety rules, and able to swim to the bank if the worst should happen . . . and that could be 50 yards/metres away through a strong current on the Thames, Shannon or Seine.

Boating offers some of the joys of camping, with an element of exploration and adventure, plus the pleasure of touring. Like camping and caravanning the worst moment is when it starts to rain and the whole family is confined in a small space with damp clothes hanging everywhere. Unlike camping it is difficult either to get away from your temporary home to a cinema or museum or to cut your losses and go home; you are committed to return your vessel to the hirer and you can get back no faster than the speed limit, the wind or your boat's engine allows. If you are on the canals or rivers you should bear this in mind when choosing where to go. A route through an urban area or along a busy waterway will provide more diversions in the way of outings ashore or waterside pubs with children's rooms.

Be prepared for the rain. Have fully waterproof clothing for deck duties and wellington boots for the mud on the towpath. Everyone should have warm nightwear and sleeping bags or duvets to make sure that they are warm for at least *part* of every 24 hours.

Even older children should have certain rules drummed into them for their own safety – and you should set an example by keeping to them too. Organise a 'man overboard' drill on Day One using a dummy (a life-jacket will do) or, if it is warm, a volunteer who can swim well. We would suggest the following rules:

● All small children and non-swimmers should wear life-jackets or a buoyancy aid at all times, even when it is hot and windless. Arm bands are not a suitable alternative.

● Everyone should wear shoes with non-slip soles at all times.

● Keep decks and passageways clear of all paraphernalia; ropes should always be coiled and stowed.

● Do not do anything which could cause you to overbalance if there is a sudden jerk; this especially means no fighting or larking about.

● Do not push the boat off with your hands or feet when entering or leaving a lock, tunnel or bridge.

● If you are on a canal or small river, keep your head below cabin top level when going under bridges.

● Under 12s should not work a lock without an adult beside him or her.

Accommodation

Boats are generally rented out by small companies. To find one consult one of the following books and brochures:

A Lazy Man's Guide to Holidays Afloat A book of hints on choosing the waterway, your craft and your itinerary. It includes lots of advertisements for hirers.

Blakes, an agency for numerous small yards with special emphasis on the Norfolk Broads. They also offer Ireland's River Shannon, the Scottish lochs, the canals and rivers of England, waterways in Holland and a number of French rivers.

Hoseasons, another agency for hirers, covering the Norfolk Broads, the canals and rivers of England and the Scottish lochs. They have a separate brochure, *Boating Holidays in France, Holland and Denmark* for those seeking a Continental holiday.

Inland Waterway Guide has a classified list of hirers on the canals and rivers plus a 'where to go' guide and lists of pubs and stopping places.

If you prefer sail to steam the yachting magazines are full of sea-going yacht charter firms. Both Hoseasons and Blakes offer sailing cruisers on the more sheltered Broads and Scottish lochs. For the less experienced, PGL Family Holidays offer flotilla sailing in the Solent and Poole Harbour. There is a skipper provided for each boat who will guide you according to your ability and, no doubt, help you in training your family to become a more effective crew.

When your crew is properly in control you might consider a flotilla holiday in Greece, Turkey or Yugoslavia with one of the many companies. Falcon offer a villa-flotilla holiday in the Greek Islands which allows you one week of beach activities, including dinghy sailing and skipper training, and one week on board your cruiser. The land-based part shares a playscheme for 5 to 13s with the dinghy sailors in Levkas so there are plenty of families on those flotillas in school holidays.

Going with babies and toddlers

The reports that we had from families with babies who tried a canal boat holiday did not recommend it. The babies slept well to the chug of the

motor but only at the expense of sleeping in a cabin full of diesel fumes, while mothers were frustrated by their inability to wash and dry clothes. Toddlers, encumbered by a harness and reins all day and swamped by even the smallest life-jacket, gave their already anxious parents an even worse time with their boredom and frustration.

The cost

Like other self-catering accommodation, you rent by the unit. If you can afford it you should look for something slightly larger than you need. A 4/6 berth cruiser could be very cramped for four adults and two children in wet weather. A 6-berth model will cost from £400 to £500 per week in August, including the flotilla holiday in the Solent. Mediterranean flotilla holidays are rather more expensive as they include air fares to your port of departure.

On top of the basic price you will have to pay for diesel fuel and, if you want one, the hire of a rowing dinghy or sail board. Life-jackets are usually provided free by the hirer.

Walking and Rambling

If you enjoy walking with groups you will find that many organised holidays of this type do not accept children under the age of 14. Three large organisations, however, are happy to welcome the whole family and it is quite possible to have a modestly priced holiday in the company of others.

Anyone who plans a walking holiday, even if they only hope to do short walks each day, should test beforehand both their children's stamina and their own ability to carry a younger child. Theoretically there is little problem taking under 2 year olds as they can be put in a baby carrier, although if you intend to walk far or if your child is over about 22 lb (10 kg) it is essential to have a good quality framed version (see page 163). However, one family told us that even with a good quality Karrimor baby carrier neither parent could manage more than half a mile each carrying an eight month old. Do not imagine that you can just put on a carrier with a heavy baby in it and stride off over the fells – it takes practice.

If you have children too small to walk the same distance as you but too large to be carried on your back, choose an HF family centre with a crèche.

If you choose a walking centre, do not worry that your family are not serious hikers as no one will mind if families with children slip off to do other things. Fellow guests and management will only resent it if you use the centre as a base from which to go on a drive every day.

The accommodation

If you want to walk with the family the following organisations offer a good choice of accommodation. Each takes bookings by the day, and in the case of Youth Hostels there may be a restriction on the length of time you may stay in each one.

Countrywide Holidays Association or CHA have 16 centres all over Britain aimed at families and groups. They are open from April to

October and children are always welcome. The centres are run as house parties, with home-cooking and a social programme in the evening. All week there are guided walks or you are free to explore the area on your own. There are several special family holidays planned during the season. In the summer they also offer holidays in France in conjunction with a similar French organisation, LVT.

HF Holidays (formerly Holiday Fellowship) have over 30 centres in Britain and Ireland offering walks graded from 1 (ascents over 2000 feet, exposed and rough walking) to 8 (under five miles on level paths and lanes). In addition, they offer a number of holidays in modest hotels in ten European countries. We received many compliments about this organisation, like 'we made lots of new friends' and 'terrific value for money'. The centres are run as a house party and have comfortable lounges and homely bedrooms with washbasins and tea-making facilities. Children are welcome at any time, although those with younger ones generally choose centres with Grade 7 and 8 walks. In the summer holiday period around 10 centres are designated for Family Holidays; a number of these are close to the sea and you can join in the walking as much or as little as you like. There is a cooperative air about child-care with parents helping each other out with baby-sitting and meal supervision. During the day there is a crèche.

Youth Hostels   There are hundreds of hostels throughout the British Isles and Europe. Excellent handbooks can be purchased giving details of the YHA (England and Wales), SYHA (Scotland), YHANI (Northern Ireland) and IYHA or An Oige (Eire). If you want to use European Hostels then you should obtain the *International Youth Hostel Handbook*, Volume 1. The handbooks are available from YHA shops in the major cities. Standards range from bare but comfortable with central heating (designated as 'special' or 'superior' in the *YHA Handbook*) to distinctly spartan (the nearest thing to a shower being the local waterfall) and designated 'simple'. Regulations vary but generally children are welcome from 5 years, but only when accompanied by an adult of the same sex. Family dormitories can be booked in advance at many hostels at the discretion of the warden. Meals are available in some hostels, while cooking facilities are offered in all. The lower grade hostels are usually closed between 10 am and 5 pm so that when the weather is poor you will be stuck out of doors. More than 20 English hostels provide family accommodation that includes special facilities for children under 5: the restricted opening hours do not apply and you usually need to book for a whole week at a time. This must be the best value self-catering accommodation to be had anywhere.

Going with babies and toddlers

The CHA and HF Holidays accept children under 2 at no charge in all centres. At the HF family centres babies and toddlers are particularly welcome; cots, high chairs, potties and buggies are provided and baby foods and disposable nappies are on sale.

With the YHA, the 'family accommodation' is tailored for you, with cots and/or high chairs available at some centres. At other hostels many wardens have children of their own, and one wrote to us to say how welcoming they are to babies and offer a cot and high chair even though they have no family accommodation.

The cost

These three organisations are non profit making and offer excellent value for what you pay. The cost of a CHA holiday is around £130 for a week's full-board in high season with 2 to 6 year olds paying 25%, 7 to 13s 50% and 14 to 17s 75%; they need not share with their parents although they will be accommodated in a room with other children. HF prices vary greatly according to the standard of the centre but are generally £140 to £200 per adult per week in August while child costs are graded by age: under 5s are free and the maximum child cost for the 14 to 16s is around £80.

The YHA, in line with its more basic facilities, is cheaper at around £60 full board for seven nights in the top quality hostels while children are charged about £10 less. Charges for other associations are broadly comparable although many do not offer meals. A small membership fee is payable to your national association: the YHA charges £11 for family membership, which covers the use of hostels world-wide.

Farm Holidays

Many farmers take in paying guests to supplement their income. The idea is that you stay in the country and see how a farm operates. From our experiences, luck in the choice of farm more than anything will determine the success of the holiday. The total number of guests will not be large. Some farms are more welcoming and less rigid about routines than others, which can make life simpler with young children. We can only stress again: telephone and discuss your requirements and choose the most pleasant and helpful host/hostess.

Your children will probably enjoy and be entertained by the animals (although they may be a little wary at first, particularly of farm dogs). They may also be interested in the machinery: a computerised milking parlour is very exciting (more so than hand milking). Nevertheless, farms can be at the end of unmade tracks which have to be negotiated on every trip out, by foot or by car. You should also be aware of the dangers of the machinery, and fields and farms can trigger off hitherto unsuspected allergies. Always take your wellingtons!

Farms either offer bed and breakfast or half-board. The facilities are not likely to be luxurious by hotel standards (you may not even have a wash basin in your room), so find out what there are and how many people will share them. On the plus side, this may mean that there are family rooms.

Farms in the British Isles

To find a farm contact the local tourist office for a list of farm accommodation or try one of the following:

B & I Line features farmhouse-centred holidays in Ireland, with inclusive ferry travel. You choose your farm from the thousand available in a special guide.

CIE offer a similar package to Ireland.

Farm Holiday Guides   There are three separate guides for England, Scotland, and Wales and Ireland, which list rural accommodation, not just on farms, county by county. They show where family rooms are available, indicate if children are welcome and what facilities there may be for little ones.

Farm & Country Holidays provides similar information on country holidays in England, Wales and Scotland.

Farm Holidays In Britain is the Farm Holiday Bureau guide in association with the ETB and uses the rocking horse symbol to show where children are welcome and if there are facilities for babies. The farm owners in England, Wales and Northern Ireland write their own entries.

Guesthouses, Farmhouses and Inns in Britain is an AA publication, showing farms, with or without family rooms, amongst the hotels and inns.

Farms abroad

You might also be interested in a farm in Europe, although their method of land cultivation could mean you will only see crops and no animals or vice versa.

Guesthouses, Farmhouses and Inns in Europe, another AA publication, lists some farmhouses in Germany and Austria.

DER *Germany and Austria* features some farm holidays which include your ferry crossing. You choose the area and a farm will be found for you.

Longship Holidays offer ferry inclusive holidays on farms in Denmark and Germany. They will match your requirements to a suitable farm (including helping out, if that is what you want).

Scanscape Holidays feature farmhouse holidays in Denmark.

Special facilities for children

In addition to the usual facilities (cots, high chairs etc.), some entries in the British guides also show whether there are sitting rooms with toys, gardens with swings, and if baby-sitting can be arranged.

The cost

You can expect to pay from about £60 per week per person for B & B in Britain. Children's reductions are available and are indicated in the guides.

The packages to Ireland and Europe will cost about £700 for two weeks for a family of four.

Skiing

Many of the hundreds of thousands of people who have enthusiastically taken to the ski slopes in the last 20 or so years will say that this is the ideal holiday for all ages, offering fresh air, exhilarating exercise, a suntan (with luck) and a much needed winter break. For most Britons it involves a week or more in the Alps or Pyrénées, although those lucky enough to live within a reasonable distance of a Scottish ski area can benefit from weekend and day trips to the slopes. As most enthusiasts take their holiday in mainland Europe, even if they manage to ski at weekends as well, this section concentrates on holidays abroad.

But what about skiing with kids? There is little doubt that it can be the ideal, although expensive, holiday for families with teenagers as it provides that promising combination of stylish outdoor sport with plenty of group activities in the evenings. For younger children the success of a skiing holiday will depend on their sportiness, how quickly they feel the cold and their attitude to going off on their own to ski classes or kindergarten.

The earliest that children are physically ready to start skiing will depend on their coordination; some say that the best guide is the child's ability to walk downstairs with only one foot at a time on each step, which will be around the fourth birthday. Even then, there is a school of thought that parents are the best teachers for pre-school children, and you will see on the slopes many Italian and French mamas tutoring their toddlers.

Accommodation

Most skiers, particularly those going to Austria and Italy, stay in a hotel. However, a significant minority choose to take an apartment or chalet with or without staff provided.

Hotels These range in price and facilities offered from the *gasthausen* of Austria, where rooms have no private facilities and dinner is taken in a nearby hotel, to comfortable international hotels with swimming pools and a choice of restaurants. A few hotels provide special facilities for small children with a crèche or kindergarten and special playroom and some of these are listed in the section on child care for non-skiing children. In some cases the crèches are for children travelling with a particular tour operator and are free to clients. If you have school age children you can join a family party in a hotel. These are offered in school holidays in various hotels and resorts by PGL, the Ski Club of Great Britain (members only) and Ski Dolphin. If you want to be sure that there will be other children around and something special provided for them to do during the holiday, Neilsons operate a 'Neilsonettes' programme for 3–8 year olds in a number of resorts. A special children's party is held each week and there may also be an evening baby-listening patrol. Wherever you decide to go, throughout the season, the resorts are filled with children.

Self-catering Increasingly, budget-minded skiers are taking self-catering holidays particularly in the purpose-built resorts in France. The accommodation on offer is not always ideal for families with younger children as a 3/4 person apartment may be one room with a rollaway bed and bunks in the lobby-cum-kitchenette. On the plus side, if you choose a modern French resort you will find that the futuristic architects have cleverly located every apartment within a snow ball's throw of the ski school and ski lifts, while supermarkets, swimming pool and restaurants can be reached under cover.

Staffed chalets mainly in France and Switzerland, which fall part way between a hotel and self-catering in terms of service, facilities and cost are very popular with British skiers. Numerous companies take over large apartments and chalets for the season, each sleeping between six and

60 people. They then re-let the unit either in its entirety to a group, or room by room, with wine and meals provided by British chalet girls. Families are welcomed by most companies when they take over a whole chalet as a group booking. Some companies, including Supertravel, John Morgan and Ski West, offer family weeks, usually in school holidays when those with children can take one or two rooms and join a party. Some companies (detailed in the section on child care for non-skiers) offer a child-minding or nanny service in certain weeks in some resorts.

Choosing a resort

In general the better the resort in terms of height and the number of runs the more expensive it will be, with a few exceptions like Gstaad that owe their place in the price hierarchy to the numbers of film stars seen on the slopes. If you are all beginners, choose a resort with limited runs and low prices – there are dozens throughout Austria.

When selecting a resort, remember that journey times from airports are quite variable and that there are several small airports actually in the mountains. Look out for flights to unusual destinations including Berne, Chambery, Grenoble, Innsbruck, Lyons and Salzburg which can cut your journey time down considerably. Otherwise choose a resort close to the major airports of Geneva and Zurich.

Lastly, when choosing where to go, look at the layout of the ski runs and the resort, using the information in a variety of brochures and the helpful maps in a skiers' guide from your library. If you are going to have to meet your children out of ski-school for lunch then you need to select a resort where you can ski a round trip of satisfying runs in two hours. You should also check that your accommodation is convenient for the ski-school or kindergarten. Remember that it will be you carrying two or more pairs of skis uphill each morning while the children complain about painful boots!

Special facilities for children

If your children are hoping to attempt a snow plough or two, but are either not yet up to your standard or you need to go to ski-school yourself, then you will find the children's classes excellent in most places. You can choose either kindergarten or ski-school depending on their age and ability.

Kindergartens take children from 3, 4 or 5 years, depending on the resort, and English is generally spoken in those resorts popular with the British. Details are provided in most brochures. They usually operate six days a week and offer supervised play and rudimentary skiing lessons with the emphasis on fun. A mid-day meal is normally provided at an extra charge but many families prefer to meet their family for lunch. The upper age limit of these groups varies considerably with children as old as 12 welcome in some resorts, while others take them no older than 6.

Ski-School   This does not offer any child care as such, just tuition for a set period each day. You simply book them in for a class and turn up on time to collect them at the end. Instructors often specialise in teaching children and yours will not be left shoulder deep in snow after a fall. Pupils are graded by ability rather than age so that a good skier aged 7 may be skiing with much older children. In some instances, outside school holidays, there may be insufficient children speaking English of comparable ability to make up even a mixed language class and your child will be better off in an adult group. If you think that turning up to meet the kids for lunch will cramp your skiing style, go with Ski Esprit or Supertravel, who arrange to meet under 14s from ski-school and supervise their lunch in a few resorts.

Taking children too young to ski

If you are an enthusiastic skier you will not want to give up just because you are now a parent. Only an innocent parent-to-be would seriously visualise themselves bombing down the pistes with baby on their back (other than on the nursery slopes on a sunny day). Babies can easily get frost-bite in that exposed position, separated from your body warmth by layers of clothing. Most of the skiing enthusiast families we know of who have small babies or toddlers take it in turns between themselves or a group of friends to care for the children or accept that one parent is not going to ski at all. There are, however, various child care schemes available if you do not mind leaving your child with a stranger, possibly with a poor command of English. These schemes include:

Public nurseries run like day nurseries where the children are cared for all day with indoor and outdoor play, meals and naps. They are usually paid for by the day or half day and pre-booking is not always required. The cost is around £10 a day with discounts for a whole week. The lower age limit at which babies and toddlers are accepted varies from nursery to nursery. The list below shows those which accept under 2s, but check the details before you book as age limits do sometimes change.

ANDORRA   Arinsal (6 months).

AUSTRIA   Brand (2 years), Gargellen (2 years), Hinterlux (2 years), Lanersbach (2 years), Lech (2 years), Oberlech (2 years), St Johann (2 years), Saalbach/Hinterglemm (2 years), Seefeld (2 years).

FRANCE   Argentière (18 months), Barèges (2 years), Chamonix (8 months), Chamonix Sud (3 months), Courcheval (2 years), Flaine (3 months), La Plagne (2 years), Les Arcs (1 year), Les Deux Alpes (6 months), Les Menuires (15 weeks), Les Orres (6 months), Meribel (2 years), Montgenèvre (18 months), Morzine (18 months), Pla d'Adet (18 months), Puy St Vincent (2 years), Risoul (6 months), St Lary (6 months), Tignes Le Lac (2 years), Tignes Val Claret (18 months), Val d'Isere (3 months), Valloire (18 months), Valmorel (6 months), Val Thorens (3 months).

ITALY   Sauze d'Oulx (6 months).

SPAIN   Formigal (6 months), Super Molina (1 year).

SWITZERLAND   Adelboden (2 years), Anzere (2 years), Crans Montana (2 months), Klosters (2 years), Les Diablerets (2 years), Murren (6 months), Verbier (18 months), Zermatt (3 months).

Mini-clubs   A few companies provide day care schemes for any of their clients staying in certain resorts. They do not offer any skiing, although the children usually get an opportunity to play outside in good weather. Ski NAT offer a mini-club in Kolsass Weer in Austria for 3 to 12 year olds which is free. Dolphin have a 'teenies club' in Les Arcs for the younger brothers and sisters of those on the family skiing holiday. Both the chalet companies Ski Esprit and Supertravel offer hotel and self-catering clients in a few resorts the use of their child minding service if space ever permits.

Chalet holidays with a nanny   Ski Esprit offer chalet parties with a qualified nanny on hand to look after children too young to go to kindergarten at no additional charge. They generally look after the children from 9 am to 2 pm, five days a week, with an option to extend cover until 5 pm at additional cost. The company is very strict about the number and ages of children cared for at the same time and we have had numerous glowing reports on the standard of care. 'The nanny looked after four 12- to 14-month-old babies together and was nothing short of superb,' said two families who shared a holiday while another was so impressed that they managed to cajole the ski-nanny to work for them once the season had ended. This service is exceedingly popular and needs to be booked before the end of the preceding July. Supertravel offers a childminder service at Verbier and Flaine for over 2s from 9 am until 4 pm, five days a week, at a cost of £6 extra per day, including lunch. Ski Val reserves four weeks in Les Arcs in the school holidays to 'Focus on the Family' when a crèche is run for the very young. Enfants Cordiales offer a small programme in one resort: children of any age are cared for in the chalet six mornings a week until 12.30. This service is free, but afternoon or evening baby-sitting costs £3 per hour per child. Small World have one chalet where child minding is offered on five days a week for under 4s, while over 4s are escorted to the local ski kindergarten. All these companies offer some evening baby-sitting.

Hotels and apartments with a crèche   There are numerous hotels which have a crèche available for hotel guests. These range from modest family run establishments to vast club complexes and vary in cost from moderate to very expensive. The following list gives most of those offered by the major tour companies. Details are in the brochures or write direct to the hotel if you plan to travel independently. Club Med, in various resorts, also operate child care schemes offering a good, but expensive, alternative to these hotels.

AUSTRIA
Bad Kleinkirchheim: Farmhouse Apartments (Yugotours).
Brand: Hotel Zaluanda, Hotel Lagant and Hotel Scesplana share a crèche in the Lagant (Blue Sky, Neilsons).
Kitzbuhel: Hotel Schloss Lebenberg (Inghams).
Lermoos: Hotel Edelweiss (Blue Sky clients only).
Schladming: Aparthotel Alpine (Blue Sky clients only).

FRANCE
Flaine: Hotel Lindars (Enterprise, Inghams, Ski West and Supertravel).
Risoul: Club Hotel (Ski Sunmed clients only).

SPAIN
Masella: Hotel Alp (Enterprise).

SWITZERLAND
Arosa: Park Hotel (Swiss Ski), Hotel Savoy, Sporthotel Valsana and Hotel Tschuggen (Inghams).
Davos: Hotel Belvedere (Inghams).
Disentis: Hotel la Cucagna and Feriencente Disentiserhof (Inghams).
Engelberg: Hotel Edelweiss (Swiss Ski).
Gstaad: Hotel Gstaaderhof (Inghams).
Interlaken (Beatenberg): Aparthotel Bluminsalp (Inghams).
Laax: Sporthotel Happy Rancho (Inghams).
Lenzerheide: Hotel Schweitzerhof and Valbella Inn (Inghams).
St Moritz: Hotel Schweitzerhof (Swiss Ski).
Wengen: Hotel Silberhorn (Swiss Ski and Supertravel), Park Hotel Beausite (Inghams).

Zermatt: Hotel Schweitzerhof (Thomson, Inghams), Mont Cervin (Swiss Ski, Inghams).

YUGOSLAVIA
Kopaonik: Hotel Baliste (Yugotours).

The cost

Skiing is an expensive holiday: the basic cost of accommodation and travel varies quite markedly through the season with prices at their highest in school holidays and at the end of February when there is the best combination of sun and snow. Prices may look attractive in the weeks before Christmas and the weeks following New Year, which may fall into your children's school holidays, but snow can be unreliable or, almost worse, be falling all day every day and be freezing cold.

The cost of the holiday will depend not just on the standard of accommodation and the season but also on the following:

Travel to the resort   Although most skiers fly, increasing numbers of companies are offering the alternative of sleeper coaches which leave various British cities on a Friday, passing through Dover in the early evening and reaching the Alps the following morning. This could save around £40 per head on a London departure and would be worth considering if you are planning a holiday with older children. If you have a large family, or are making up a party, you may choose to drive, particularly if you have selected one of the many resorts in the French Alps or Rhône Valley which can be reached on snow-free motorways in 10 to 12 hours from Calais. As a self drive holiday costs some £80 less per head than an air holiday then a family of five should be more than compensated for the cost of the ferry (at offpeak rates) and motoring expenses.

Ski and boot hire around £15–£30 for a week per person.

Ski tuition   £20–£40 depending on the number of hours each day.

Ski lifts for which even beginners should allow at least £20. More experienced skiers who might expect to pay up to around £65 for a week's use of the lifts in a top class resort can take advantage of special family rates in certain resorts. In Verbier up to two children under 16 can ski at no cost if both parents buy passes, while a family with two 16–25 year olds can buy four passes for the price of three. A number of resorts offer

Discounts on Skiing Holidays Winter 1986/7

The following discounts apply to holidays lasting for one week; sometimes you will get a better deal if you go for two weeks. Please note that many hotels and chalets have rooms suitable for four beds. The table applies to children sharing a room with two adults unless otherwise stated.

Company	Discount for first child	Discount for second child	Qualifying age	Notes
Best	Free or 10–50%		2–11	
Bladon Lines Chalets	Prices from £120	Prices from £120	2–15	One child price holiday per adult.
Bladon Lines Self-catering	Prices from £110	Prices from £110	2–15	One child price holiday per adult.
Blue Sky	10–50% off Up to 25% off	10–50% off Up to 25% off	2–5 6–11	
Enfants Cordiales	50% off 25% off	50% off 25% off	2–5 6–13	Own room discount 25% for 2–13s. Under 2s pay £45 to include crèche.
Enterprise	15–60% off	15–60% off	2–11	In apartments there must be maximum occupancy. Subsequent children get 10% off.
Horizon Hotels	Free or 15–50% off	10–30% off	2–10	Children in their own room get 10–25% off.
Horizon Apartments	10–30% off	10–30% off	2–10	Must be maximum occupancy.

Inghams Hotels	15–35% off	15–35% off	2–11	The higher discount applies at all times outside Christmas and half-term holidays.
Intasun Skiscene	Free or up to 40% off	20% off	2–12	Child price applies to any number of children in apartments.
Neilson	Free or 10–50% off	10% off	2–11	All children not sharing with parents get 10% discount.
Ski Esprit	Free or 15–50% off Free or 10–40% off Free or 5–30% off	15–50% off 10–40% off 5–30% off	2–5 6–13 14–15	For all age groups children in their own room get half the discount. Infants charged £40 to include crèche.
Ski NAT	Free or 10–50% off	10% off	2–11	
Ski Sunmed	10–30% off	Nil	2–11	
Swiss Travel Service	40% off	40% off	2–11	Children occupying their own room each receive a discount of £50.
Thomas Cook	Free or 10–75% off 15%	10–75% off 15%	2–11 Students	Discount applies to students sharing with one another.
Thomson	15–50% off	Up to 50% off	2–11	
Yugotours	30% off	30% off	2–10	

free skiing to younger children: with, for example, no charge for under 7s in Avoriaz, under 6s in Mayrhofen and under 5s in Brand, Tignes and Val d'Isere.

Drinks and snacks   Most drinks, lunches and incidental items are expensive. Your children will be hungry in the fresh mountain air so you will need to budget for a hot meal at mid-day.

Clothing and accessories   It is essential for everyone to have sufficient warm waterproof clothing or else the holiday will be a nightmare. It is usually not worth hiring ski suits even for growing children because the cost is very high. Try C & A or Asda for good value new clothes, or the notice board of your local dry ski slope for second-hand items.

There are fairly good discounts on package deals available for children, if you shop around, not only among the larger companies. Some free holidays are available for early bookers but generally at times when snow is less reliable. In 1986/7 the following companies were offering free places, although the number of weeks and resorts varies considerably: Best, Horizon, Intasun Skiscene, Neilsons, Ski Esprit, Ski NAT and Thomas Cook.

The brochures of the companies listed on pages 116–117 offer the best discounts for at least one of the age groups shown. All discounts apply to children sharing a room with two adults except for the student discount offered by Thomas Cook when each student in the room can claim.

Holidays for Unaccompanied Children

Unaccompanied holidays for children, many in the style of the American Summer Camp are the great growth market of recent years. Increasing numbers of two working parents, who do not want to leave their children kicking their heels during the school holidays, has fuelled the growth.

Once your child is about 7, there may be opportunities to go away on organised holidays through a group or school. Unless a child is a Brownie, Cub or a member of a church fellowship, you may have to arrange such a holiday yourself through the PTA or church. For an older child, you might organise an overseas exchange visit, either through the school, personal contacts or an agency like the Robertson Organisation which pairs up English and French, German and Spanish children between 11 and 18 years. If you are interested in a foreign exchange contact the Central Bureau for Educational Visits and Exchanges.

There is a wide range of holiday and day camps if you want something with more scope or less educational. The day camps are considered here with the residential holidays as the same points apply to both. Your choice may depend partly on whether you live within striking distance of a centre taking daily campers.

Day camps take children from 3 years old, while residential holidays take them from the age of 6 years. You will know whether your own child is ready to venture away from home so young, but we would have some doubts about sending an under 5, who gets exhausted after two or three hours of playgroup or nursery school, off for an eight-hour day of travel and activities. But on the other hand, in the event of a family crisis, your 6-year-old may be better off on a residential holiday than being cared for at home by a group of neighbours. And although we think these ages a little extreme, the youngest of three children whose brother and sister are going to camp may not agree with us.

Any holiday is likely to be more successful for younger children if they go with a friend or member of the family, particularly if they have to travel to the centre by group transport. It is rather like starting at a new school and thus a bit nerve-racking the first time.

Choosing a holiday

Ensure that all your requirements will be met before you make a firm booking. You might ask the following questions:

● *Is the subject of a specialist holiday going to be taught to a satisfactory standard for your children's needs?* If they are already good sailors do not send them on a general water sports holiday but to a specialist sailing school. Similarly, is there sufficient equipment to keep them occupied, or will they always be waiting for their turn? Are the activities available on the main site or will they have to travel by coach, perhaps as far as 15 miles, to find suitable facilities?

● *What happens when it rains?* Is there a wet weather programme or will you be paying money to have your child entertained by a video while it pours down outside?

● *Will your child be of comparable age to others in the group?* It can be difficult to make friends with those much older or much younger. Similarly, if your child minds, you should ensure that others are of the same sex (particularly important where a subject appeals more to one sex than the other) and that the group is not dominated by foreign children. What size are the groups?

● *Are there facilities to phone home?* Particularly necessary if your children are likely to get homesick.

● *Will the food appeal to your children if they are fussy?* If the answer is no, they may be better off at a day camp where they can take their own sandwiches. Will you have to pay extra for the food? Will it be hot? And will there be enough of it?

● *Are you happy with the standards of safety, hygiene and medical care?* For a candid answer you need to talk to someone whose children have been before or, better still, pay a visit beforehand. Camps do not need to be registered and there are no obligatory standards of care required. There is now a British Activity Holiday Association and they will have guidelines, but this still does not ensure that every sailing instructor insists on life-jackets or that each camp operates a fire drill. You should look for staff ratios of one to every five children and you should expect a nurse to be in attendance.

Multi-activity holidays

Most children, and particularly those under 12, will go on a multi-activity holiday or camp. They are generally held in boarding schools with their own playing fields, swimming pools and sports halls. The programme will include every sport from archery to volley ball interspersed with more unusual activities like Frisbee Golf, Ballpond (swimming in a pool of 20,000 balls!) and raft building. There may also be quieter options including video film making, drama, and arts and crafts. They are generally for the sports-minded, active child and could prove to be purgatory for the 'head in a book' type.

Special interest holidays

You will find brochures of the children's activity holiday specialists full of single subject holidays for those aged over 7, including computing, cricket, cycling, fantasy world, fishing, motor sport, mountain walking, ponies and horses, soccer, tennis, theatre and water sports, among others. If you are concerned about forthcoming exam results your child can even go to 'Swot Camp' to brush up on maths and French.

There are numerous specialist centres for single activities, not solely for children but with special weeks for young holidaymakers. These include water sports instruction, pony trekking, equestrian skills, sports coaching, game fishing, mountain walking, ocean-going yachting, music and theatre. For details look at the publications on page 94 under Activity and Hobby Holidays, several of which have a section on holidays for children.

DAY CAMPS

Springing up around every major city are day camps run by the children's holiday specialists and by public schools offering the use of their facilities. They can be a solution to the problem of school holiday blues.

The cost is in the region of £75 for the first week and £45 for subsequent weeks excluding transport to and from camp each day. Although this may seem expensive the ratio of counsellors to children should be one to five, and there are excellent facilities. Some activities cost extra, like trial bikes and horse riding, not to mention insurance, so the bill could reach three figures for one week.

It is impossible to list all the centres, but in 1986 they served London and the surrounding area, as well as Birmingham, Bristol, Eastbourne, Edinburgh, Reading, Leeds and Manchester (South). Escorted transport is usually available from the catchment area at a fixed rate regardless of the length of the trip. You may find that if you have two children or there are other campers living nearby, it is cost effective to send them by minicab or taxi, depending on distance, or to organise a car pool. However, one 5 year old said that the bus trip was the best bit!

The following companies operate more than one camp with at least 20 activities to choose from at each:

Camp Beaumont takes 3 to 15 year olds at about 10 centres offering a wide multi-activity programme. Nursery Camp is the special programme for 3 to 5 year olds.

Dolphin Adventure takes 3 to 14 year olds at over 15 centres. These are mainly multi-activity camps but children can also select Grand Prix camps. The Teenies (under 7s) have a special programme.

PGL welcomes daily campers at 10 of their residential centres all round England starting from 6 years old.

RESIDENTIAL HOLIDAYS IN BRITAIN

Many companies offer holidays for unaccompanied children, and of these the following have two or more centres offering a range of activities. For single centre organisations and companies with more than one centre, but a limited range of pursuits, read the Activity Holiday handbooks listed on page 94.

Costs vary with the activities selected and the age of the child, but as a general guide a multi-activity one week holiday will cost £160 to £170 with subsequent weeks at £120 each. In addition the child will need pocket money and there will be extra trips and activities to budget for.

Allnatt Activity Holidays at two permanent centres for 9 to 18 year olds. Multi-activity only with around 30 options.

Ardmore Adventure Holidays marketed by Hoseasons Holidays at four centres operate in the Easter and half-term holidays as well as during the summer for 4 to 16 year olds. Multi-activity with around 40 options, plus specialist tennis and computing courses.

Camp Beaumont has about 12 centres all round Britain offering holidays for 7 to 16 year olds. These are multi-activity holidays with around 100 options (including the best range of arts & crafts) and specialist holidays for computer enthusiasts, sportsmen, swots and potential stars of stage and screen.

Dolphin Adventure has around 10 centres for 7 to 17 year olds. Multi-activity holidays with about 60 options and specialist holidays for water sports enthusiasts, horse lovers, potential adventurers, spook seekers and sportsmen.

PGL Adventure Holidays has around 30 centres taking 6 to 18 year olds. Multi-activity holidays are banded by age (16–18s, 12–16s, 8–13s and 6–9s) to ensure children are not out of their depth, and offer around 40 activities. Specialist holidays include stage, computing, motor sports, cycling, water sports of all sorts, pony trekking and mountain adventure training.

UNACCOMPANIED HOLIDAYS ABROAD

These holidays usually have a strong theme although if you want a general tour PGL does a French Explorer Holiday based near Rouen. The following are just some of the trips offered by the major companies:

Canal Boats

PGL runs a holiday on a 28-berth barge in Holland for 12 to 18 year olds. The week-long trip takes in Amsterdam, Delft and Gouda.

Canoeing

PGL offers a canoeing holiday on the River Ardèche in Central France, one of the great scenic attractions of Europe. The children, between 13 and 17 years, live in two-person tents with meals cooked for them.

Skiing

This is one of the most popular trips for unaccompanied youngsters. Prices are usually 'all in', to include ski and boot hire, lessons and sometimes the lift pass, as well as all meals. Holidays are offered by a number of operators including:

Dolphin takes 12 to 17 year olds to three centres.

John Morgan offers Teens Ski Weeks for 14 to 17 year olds in one resort at Easter.

Neilson with teenage weeks in two Austrian resorts for 13 to 17 year olds.

PGL takes teenagers to three resorts.

Ski Club of Great Britain offers 'young members' parties for 9 to 15 year olds and 16 to 18 year olds. You must be a member of the Club to join a party or even to see details of the programme.

Ski MacG reserves a number of weeks for young people on their own. There are Kids' Weeks for 8 to 12s and Teenagers' Weeks for 13 to 16 year olds.

Supertravel operates an unescorted teenagers' party to two resorts in the school holidays.

Windsurfing and dinghy sailing

PGL operates a holiday on the Mediterranean coast of France for budding windsurfers and aspiring dinghy sailors in their fleet of 'Toppers'.

One-Parent Holidays

This section is not only aimed at single parents, who may have a special need for company in a similar social situation, but also at those who can get away for a break more frequently than their partner and who have the simple choice of a holiday alone or no holiday at all.

Mothers often like to take advantage of the years when they are not tied to restricted annual leave to get away on their own; visits to friends and relatives top the list, followed by holiday cottages (particularly in the Easter holidays when friends can afford to lend them or rental charges are modest) and camping.

How easy it is to cope with taking children on your own depends on the number of children you have. At best, with just one child of whatever age, it will be manageable, although you will have to ensure that they have company of similar age (or a doting grandmother) if they are not going to drive you mad with their boredom. The greater the number of children, the more sensible it is to go somewhere with other adults on hand to help, at least in emergencies. If you cope at home as a single parent, you probably have friends, neighbours or relatives who will lend a hand if a child is rushed to hospital, for example, so think carefully about isolating yourself from the world if you are holidaying on your own.

However many children you have, travelling on your own has pitfalls. You will already know how difficult it can be to drive alone with a small child or children, even for a short distance. If you plan to go by car think about travelling at night, if your children can be depended upon to sleep. With two or more young ones you will find yourself frustrated by never being able to leave them for a moment while you go and buy drinks or tickets, and every time one wants to go to the loo you will all have to go.

Special holidays for single parents

Some parents want to get together with other single parents and have fun in the same way that any group of single people would on holiday. You will not find these holidays dominated by mothers. Many fathers, separated from their children by divorce, do not have a suitable home to which the children can go for a fortnight's access, so they take the opportunity to give the children a holiday instead.

Two non-profitmaking organisations offer special holidays for one parent families:

OPF Holidays (One Parent Family Holidays) was formed in 1975 by lone parents to offer others in a similar situation the chance of a Continental holiday. The venues change each year so that repeat clients have a different choice range. The programme may include coach holidays to a camp site on the French Riviera, air holidays to caravans in Italy, apartments on the Costa Brava, hotels in Majorca and Greece and weekend breaks by ferry to Brittany. Each of these destinations may be offered only once or twice in a season so you cannot choose your resort and the date of travel. During the whole season there are OPF holidays to a caravan holiday park in Bude, at which you can camp as well. Prices are modest and quite specifically geared towards single parents. One parent with two children could go to a caravan on the French Riviera for a week at Easter for just over £200 or to a tent in high summer for a fortnight for £450.

SPLASH (Single Parent Links And Special Holidays, formerly Gingerbread Holidays) offer a good range of breaks in the UK and Europe at a low cost. They offer holiday centres run by Butlin's, Haven, Leisure, Pontin's and Warner as well as some independent centres. If you prefer a hotel they offer a few for a week or a weekend break but the cost puts it beyond the reach of the average single parent. For those who can afford them there are some holidays further afield, but the choice is limited. A family of three could have a half-board holiday at Butlin's for £105 for a week or a caravan holiday in Bude for just over £60, but you are expected to go outside school holidays to secure these deals and they offer virtually nothing which does not require you to take your child out of school in June or September.

Other holidays

Some one-parent families, and those other parents holidaying on their own, prefer something which allows a better chance to socialise than a self-catering holiday.

Most people will be reluctant to pay a hotel or tour operator for two adult spaces before they can benefit from child discounts (or free holidays). Otherwise a holiday for one parent and two children costs exactly the same as a holiday for two parents and one child. In most places the best discount you are likely to get will be the adult paying full rate plus a single room supplement, and then having to share that single room with the child or children receiving discount. In this situation you may find that for only a slightly higher cost you could simply pay the full adult price for your first child and stay in a double room far more comfortably.

The following are just some of the companies which in 1986 were offering a favourable deal to parents on their own. In addition, if you are holidaying in Britain, look at the *Jonathan Lewis Family Holiday Guide* which shows in its classified listings where single parent families enjoy the normal discounts for children.

Arrow Villas and Apartments   At least £25 discount is allowed at the rate of one child per adult (Spain, Canary Islands, Malta and Portugal).

Arrowsmith   Child discount of up to 50% given at the rate of one child per adult (Spain and Balearics, Canary Islands, Portugal and Greece).

Beach Villas   Reduction for children at the rate of one child per adult on self-catering holidays up to 50% and a minimum of £30 off per child (Spain and Balearics, Canary Islands, Greece, Italy and Corsica).

Cosmos 10–50% off for one child 2–16 sharing with one parent in Sol Hotels (Spain and Balearics, Canary Islands).

Enterprise Free place or 10–50% off for first child and 10–50% off for second child in Sol Hotels for single parents (Spain and Balearics and Canary Islands).

HF Holidays All children pay the concessionary price, i.e. under 5s free, 5–9 £40, 10–13 £55, 14–16 £80 (Britain).

Lancaster Family First apartment holidays. 25% off for the first child and 20% for second and subsequent children in April, May and October (Spain and Balearics, Canary Islands, Portugal, Italy and Greece).

Multitours Their flat rate and free holidays in hotel accommodation apply to single parent families, but meals must be paid for as taken (Malta and the Algarve).

Pontin's In May, June, early July and September, children 2–9 at the rate of one child per adult are offered free full-board holidays (Britain).

Starvillas All children 2–16 receive £25–50 off their villa holiday with the reduction depending on season (Greece, Spain, Corsica and Portugal).

Sunmed – Go Greek Single parent families booking before early January are entitled to a 50% discount on the first child's holiday (Greece).

Thomson Most Sol Hotels give 15–30% off for the first child in single parent families and 10% off for subsequent children (Spain and Balearics, Canary Islands).

Thomson Small & Friendly 15% off all children's holidays at all times, one child to one parent, and no need to share a room; in Austria and the Italian Lakes this discount rises to 25% for most of the season (Spain and Balearics, Greece, Italy, Portugal and Austria).

Timsway Reductions at the rate of one child per adult, so that single parents receive full child discounts, i.e. up to 25% off (mainly Greece).

Tjaereborg Single parents receive 10% off for the first child and the normal child discount for the second, i.e. up to 35% off (Spain and Balearics, Canary Islands, Portugal and Greece).

Yugotours   Discounts of 30–40% are given all season to one child sharing with one adult (Yugoslavia).

Holidaying With a Disabled Person

If someone in your family is disabled and this is your first holiday together you could start by contacting the association concerned with the disability and your local social services department. Both may organise holidays and will certainly be able to offer advice. One of the best sources of holiday suggestions will be similarly placed friends.

Many of the holiday operators mentioned in this book have special facilities for the disabled. Thomson, for example, invite you to telephone their client service department for advice. Contact any of the operators or follow up any ideas that appeal to you and discuss your family's needs and requirements early on in making your holiday arrangements. All those involved with holidays for the disabled stress how important this is. There are two very good books available to help you with all aspects of your holiday. These are:

Holidays for Disabled People published by RADAR is packed with information (amongst the ads) about holidays in Britain and tells you how to get abroad with the aid of your travel agent. There are some organisations mentioned in it which provide family accommodation, e.g. Arthritis Care, Break, The British Polio Fellowship, John Groom's Association for the Disabled and Mencap.

Travellers' Guide for the Disabled from the AA, includes comprehensive information on facilities at AA approved British hotels, detailed itineraries in Europe and lists AA recommended self-catering properties, camping and caravanning sites that can cater for the needs of the disabled. You would need to check with the proprietor in all cases whether children are welcome.

Travelling with the disabled brings its own complications. Both British Rail and the Civil Aviation Authority produce their own useful leaflets. Concessionary fares are available from British Rail (Disabled

Persons Railcard), and the ferry companies through membership of the Disabled Drivers' Association or the Disabled Drivers' Motor Club.

The accommodation

If you fear social isolation or would prefer the support of others similarly placed around you, this can be provided by some organisations, but the accommodation may not be aimed at a family which might include two or three boisterous able-bodied children in addition to the person with special needs. If you use the following sources, you should be able to identify places where the whole family is welcome.

All ETB publications use a disabled welcome symbol which, used in conjunction with the children welcome symbol, might achieve your ends.

Camping for the Disabled provides lists of accessible camp sites in France, Switzerland and West Germany (SAE for all enquiries).

Intervac, a home swapping agency, identifies properties suitable for the disabled.

The Good Holiday Cottage Guide, the Forestry Commission's *Get Away To It All* and Blake's *Country and Seaside Holidays*, self-catering, all indicate where access is available for the physically disabled.

The Holiday Care Service is a registered charity which provides a personalised information and advice service on holidays in Britain and abroad for people with special needs.

Home Swapping

Can you imagine a way to holiday anywhere in the world, just for the cost of the travel? A house swap can mean just that. You exchange your house or flat for someone else's, and the other family comes and lives in yours. You can exchange everything, even cars, home-helps, pets, bills and, of course, the kitchen sink. In Britain, where you might swap one suburban street for another, you will have a new area's supply of free or cheap entertainment to explore. Don't worry that your house is not grand enough or that your area isn't a tourist haunt. We know of one family in a not very exciting estate house in a not very exciting part of Berkshire (no public transport for miles and no local shops) who have successfully swapped for years, including visits to the USA and Italy. After all, the idea of staying in someone else's home is more attractive to many committed self-caterers than using a holiday let where the furniture may be elderly and the utensils of limited use to anyone. Home exchangers look after the property they borrow as they know you are in theirs, and also you do not have the worry of leaving your house unoccupied during your absence.

How to go about it

On a simple level, swap with friends or relatives. However, there are pitfalls to the DIY arrangement, such as relatives upsetting your neighbours. We would recommend that you look for swapping mates through one of the following agencies:

Global Home Exchange & Travel Service is a New England based company with a representative in London. You send £25 and 10–12 colour photos of the inside and outside of your house together with details of what you require and what you can offer. They then match you up with an exchange in your specified area within Europe or the States, and you pay an additional fee of £125 upon acceptance of this exchange partner.

Home Interchange is a long-established British company. For a £20 membership fee you will receive their directory which offers exchanges in Canada, USA, Western Europe and some Commonwealth countries.

InterService Home Exchange is an American company with a strong demand for home exchanges in England. They only deal in dollars or International Money Orders so are probably best used for your US exchange. The membership fee is $24 for their directory.

Intervac is another long-established British company which will send you three directories a year for the membership fee of £25. They list exchangers in Europe, Scandinavia, Ireland, Israel and USA. They provide lots of helpful information to ensure a successful exchange.

N.C.T. House Swap Register offers exchanges in Britain. You can be sure that all the families have children. The list costs £3 and all profits go to the National Childbirth Trust.

Worldwide Home Exchange Club is an American company with a British representative. They 'trade homes' in 30 different countries. A membership fee of £15 will secure the directory.

Most of the directories are produced early in the year with some companies supplying updates. Although early membership will possibly give you more choice, you can still look for an exchange partner later on without your details being available to others. All the directories list the properties with a comprehensive language of abbreviations to identify amenities and facilities. You will normally be charged an extra £5 for the reproduction of a photograph of your home. You do all the work to find your swapping mate from the thousands available (except with Global).

Swapping tips

● Try to exchange with people with similar aged children so that any equipment you require, suitable toys and books should be provided.

● Exchange as much information beforehand as you can so that, hopefully, no problems will arise during your swap. You will feel happier leaving your house with others after correspondence as they will no longer seem like total strangers.

● Undertake your first exchange with someone who has done this before, and also try to arrange an overlap for a short time at the beginning so that you actually meet and sort out difficulties.

● Remember that others' expectations may be different to yours. For instance, Americans often do not realise how small everything will be!

● Make sure that swappers are insured properly, and clear the situation with your house and car insurance company. If your company car is not exchangeable, you may need to hire another.

● Put away anything valuable or anything you are especially concerned about.

● Ask British Telecom to bill separately for a set period, if you are worried about long distance calls. You may find your swappers more extravagant with heating and hot water than you are.

● Make up an information pack with precise details on, say, the quirks of your washing machine or oven, and include information on where-abouts of stopcocks and restaurants, etc. All the agencies suggest what information to include.

● Clear out space in drawers and cupboards for their clothes and food, and leave a 'welcome pack' for their first meal in your house and their homecoming meal when you leave theirs.

● Think about all the work you will have to do before you go. One mother said that her house had never been so clean before!

● Think about pet and garden care arrangements. Do your swappers really want to spend all their time preventing the weeds from over-running your garden? Do you want to spend all your time looking for their cat?

Special facilities for children

You will have to arrange for any equipment you need to be provided, or be clear what you will need to take. Why not arrange for your exchangers to use your baby-sitting circle or give them the name of your regular sitter? Consider giving families with teenagers the names and phone numbers of other similar aged youngsters so that they can be introduced to the local scene. You could also rope in friends and relatives to provide a bit of hospitality.

The cost

Apart from the membership fee, you will need to budget for postage and stationery. You need to send out an enquiry letter and further details plus a photograph to anyone you are remotely interested in. This could mean anything up to 50 or 60 letters plus stamps by the time you have completed the arrangement. Remember that home swapping could entail renewal of your domestic equipment. ('We've got to replace the toaster before the Americans come.') You will need to ensure that all your insurance needs are met. The most major item of holiday expenditure will be your travel costs, but you could make substantial savings on your fares to Europe by exchanging cars.

General Hints

If you have young children or a baby and have not tackled a holiday as a family before, you will be surprised at all the things you have to think about. The following are hints for you to go through well in advance. They are geared to holidays abroad as these require most preparation.

Try to find out as much as you can beforehand about the area you will be visiting. The children, especially those of school age, could do the same and you should enlist the aid of teachers, friends and relatives in sparking interest and giving information. There are many aspects which can be explored: historical, geographical, marine, and so forth.

Show pre-school children pictures and read them stories about where you are going; tell them what they can do and see on holiday and how they will get there. If they are very small, do this only shortly before you go as time spans will confuse them.

Some children might be encouraged to write a diary whilst away including items such as shells or tickets. Similarly, on return you could use some of your holiday pictures and souvenirs to help your child make a book so that new facts and experiences are better remembered and the story can be shown to friends and relatives.

WHAT TO DO WELL IN ADVANCE

Passports

All children, including newborn babies, should have either their own passport or be entered on one, or preferably both, of their parents'. One family had a ruined holiday when Mum had to return 10 days early to see her ailing grandmother, with three very disgruntled children in tow as they were only on her passport. As soon as your children reach their sixteenth birthday, they will need their own passports. The passport application form CAF is available from Post Offices; the process can take a long time in high season. A British Visitor's passport is available from Post Offices, valid for one year, but check that it is valid for the country you are visiting. It would not be acceptable in the USA or in Morocco, for instance. Morocco also requires you to affix a photo of your children endorsed by the Passport Office. Visas are required for some East European countries, the USA and other faraway places; check with your travel agent. Also check whether visas are required if you are travelling on a non-British passport.

Vaccinations

If you are travelling beyond northern Europe you may need vaccinations. See the section on Health.

Money

Travellers' cheques, foreign currency, Eurocheques plus Eurocards all need to be ordered well in advance, unless you want to spend your last few days dashing to and from your bank. Credit cards are the one method that needs no prior organisation.

Holiday insurance

If you are holidaying in Britain the only insurance you may need is for cancellation. If you are going abroad, holiday insurance is strongly advised and should include cancellation (which is relatively cheap), medical expenses and loss or damage to belongings (if you do not already have cover under an existing medical plan and an all-risks house insurance). According to your family's needs, you might also consider protection against travel or luggage delay and cover against the costs of alternative travel arrangements if you miss your plane or ship.

Try to buy your insurance cover when you book the holiday as half of the claims arise because a trip has to be cancelled due to unforeseen events.

Most holiday insurance cover is offered by the tour operators, which may appear compulsory. If this insurance does not cover what you want you should see your insurance broker about an alternative or top-up policy. Should there be insufficient detail about the policy in the brochure, ask for further information before you make your booking and the policy comes into effect. Scrutinise the limits you are able to claim under each section, e.g. £250 for money lost, and check on how much excess is charged for any claim. Also note what exclusion clauses there are, e.g. illness arising from pregnancy may not be covered even if the pregnancy started after taking out the policy. Hazardous activities may be excluded too.

Take all your holiday insurance policies with you (leaving a record at home) and keep evidence of any reclaimable expenses. Besides financial ruin, you can risk delays in treatment without a certified copy of the policy. Property losses should be reported to the local police within 24 hours. Nearly every policy includes words to the effect that 'lack of proper care towards your luggage could well prejudice any claim.' So expect the insurers to be markedly unsympathetic to a claim for lost property if, for example, your teenagers left the camera unguarded on the beach for three hours.

Unfortunately, discounts for children are not common although many companies make no charge for under 2s, and with some under 4s are free. You should shop around for a policy which will suit your family at the most reasonable price. Bargains exist if you look around carefully. BUPA subscribers can take their first child at half premium and any other children free even if the family is not normally covered. Some discounts are not worth having if the basic charge is already high. In general the cost for an adult for a fortnight's holiday in Europe varies from £14 to £20 for an inclusive package holiday (the higher rate being for skiing).

Motor insurance

Motoring risks are usually covered by a Green Card – an extension obtained on your UK car insurance – and by special breakdown insurance. In Spain you will also require a Bail Bond.

Medical insurance

Beware, some of the comprehensive policies have low medical cover. You should not settle for less than £100,000 and full payment of all hospital costs if going to Europe. You should also ensure that the foreign hospital will invoice your insurer directly. Check that you are free to use any doctor or hospital of your choice. 'Approved' medical facilities can prove disastrous in an emergency.

If you are taken ill or have an accident abroad full costs for treatment in another country can be astronomical. Whilst the British government has reciprocal health care arrangements with the countries in the EEC and some others, these may not be as comprehensive as those provided under the NHS and, in our opinion, the money saved on premiums is not worth all the lengthy procedures involved. You obtain form SA30 'Medical treatment during visits abroad' from the local DHSS office, complete form CM1 and apply for Certificate E111 which you will need to show for treatment. You will generally still have to pay the doctor on the spot and claim from a local insurance office for a refund within ten days. At the end of all this, you may not receive a full refund. You can consider extending your personal health insurance, if you have it, but check that it covers all costs such as travel to hospital.

WHAT TO DO A FEW WEEKS BEFOREHAND

Keep calm and make lots of lists: who will feed the goldfish, a reminder to cancel the milk and papers, who to leave your house keys and your holiday address with, who will push the circulars properly through the letter box . . . ?

Make lists of what you will need to pack and start borrowing, whether skiing clothes or a portable high chair. Start stocking up: you could prepare your holiday medical kit (see the section on Health), collect your

suntan preparations, put together your photographic equipment and organise the following:

Prepare a laundry kit   Buy some concentrated detergent such as *Dylon Travelwash*; pegs, string and a nailbrush or small scrubbing brush might be useful. If you are going to the coast, it may be polluted by tar so buy a dry cleaning kit to take with you to the beach (not in an aerosol can if you are flying). You may be able to buy tar remover at the larger resorts.

Prepare a mending kit   Include an all-purpose pair of scissors.

Prepare a package of pastimes   Bearing in mind the weather, select books, tapes, cardboard models, activity packs and put them away so that they will be fresh and not played with beforehand. For older children, borrow a large jigsaw or some different board games. (See the section on Entertainment in Travelling Hints.)

Prepare your reference books   Take any that you might need, such as books on flora, shells, fungi and insects.

If you have a baby or toddler, think about all you will need (see the section on Holidaying with a Baby or Toddler).

WHAT TO DO WHEN YOU ARRIVE

Check that all the facilities are as promised and are in order.

Safety

Local hazards   Check that the environment is safe, particularly for smaller children and babies. Children do not have your experience and will not appreciate potential dangers like sharp cacti. Find out about steps, roads, pools and other hazards. Ask whether the local beaches are totally safe or whether there are strong currents or jellyfish.

Beds   Bunk beds should have a safety rail on the upper bed but there should not be too great a gap between this and the mattress or the child may slip down between them and be caught by the head and choke.

Cots   Parents whose children are using cots should see the section on babies and toddlers.

Balconies Examine your balcony for space under and between the bars and, if it is hazardous, ask to be moved to the ground floor.

Lifts Check that the lifts are safe if your children are old enough to work them by themselves. Three-sided lifts are quite common in even fairly modern hotels in Spain and older hotels in France and you would be foolhardy to let your charges ever use them unaccompanied.

Windows If you are in the upper storey fasten them with string if they are low enough for your small child to open and fall out of.

Glass Are there any plate glass patio doors your child might run into? Make them noticeable with masking tape.

Electrical Light switches on the Continent are set at lower levels and sockets are often in tempting positions. In one case we heard of, the cot was pushed up against the socket – perfect for poking at through the bars. Luckily, this Mum had some very sticky luggage labels, issued by the travel company, which she stuck over the top. Abroad you will often find no pullcords and electric switches placed neatly next to washbasins.

Local facilities

Baby-sitting Ask about the facilities available – it is best to try and find someone who speaks a little English – and discover the rate, which tends to be more expensive abroad. One family found that a baby-sitter in Switzerland wanted £2 an hour *per child* (for four children), not £2 per hour in total as implied by the tourist office. Always tell the sitter where you will be.

Rainy (and dry) day activities Visit the tourist office to find out about any interesting events occurring during your stay, such as local carnivals, and about children's facilities like special boat trips and playgrounds. Make a mental note of suitable activities for wet days.

If abroad, be sure you have the name of an English-speaking doctor.

WHAT TO DO WHILST YOU ARE THERE

Start the siesta habit from Day One if you want your children to stay up with you in the evening. In Europe you can benefit from time changes:

the child who sleeps 7 pm to 7 am in Britain may be persuaded to sleep 8 pm to 8 am on holiday with no change in routine!

Rules Make any that are necessary in the new environment as soon as possible. It will be too late to introduce them after your child has set off down the road from the unfenced garden.

Water safety Remind your family about simple safety precautions every time you come into contact with outdoor water, whether at the seaside or if you are just going fishing. Avoiding danger is vital in preventing accidents; children who are able to swim well in an indoor pool are often over-confident, and this, combined with ignorance of potential dangers such as strong currents or weeds and the 'chill factor', can be lethal. Instil in your family the following rules:

● Very young children must be watched closely at all times near water. This includes small amounts of water such as ornamental ponds as well as swimming pools, river banks and the sea.

● Do not let anyone play on inflatable mattresses or boats in the sea or rivers without supervision. If in any doubt at all about the wind or currents, tie a cord to the toy and hold it while the kids play.

● Rubber rings and armbands are only buoyancy aids and proper life-jackets should be worn for canoeing and sailing.

● Do not allow diving into unfamiliar water; you can be maimed for life, or worse, if you hit a rock or the bottom sooner than expected.

● No one should swim for at least an hour after a meal.

● Anyone complaining of feeling tired, cold or ill should leave the water immediately and change into dry clothes. In cold weather you should carry a thermos with a hot drink to warm children up after a dip or boating.

Eating out Do not worry about taking children to restaurants in holiday areas: everyone does it. In British resorts meals are generally served in the early evening, whilst in southern Europe there is nothing peculiar about the whole family eating out late. Don't be surprised if your children go off their food in restaurants even if they normally eat goulash and ratatouille with relish at home. A week of what they fancy will not do them much harm. If you are staying in a hotel where your room is near the restaurant, you could try feeding the children on the starter courses and then ask the waiter to hold your main course or dessert while one of you puts them to bed.

Label your children with their names and the address of where you are staying if you visit a crowded carnival or show and they are too young to know what to do if they get lost.

Holiday representatives on site can be helpful. Use them.

Travelling Hints

Wherever you choose to take a holiday, a journey will mark the beginning and the end of it. This section aims to help you alleviate the stress and avoid potential disasters, such as a normally responsible 6 year old who wanders out into the middle of a busy road after a four-hour car journey. After a long journey your child could be disorientated, whichever way you travel.

The longer your journey, the better the facilities provided at terminals, with the notable exception of night trains in Europe. Food obtained in transit will be relatively expensive and not necessarily to your taste, so it is worth taking sandwiches.

By the end of the jouney your children may be tired and bad-tempered as well as dirty and sticky. And you may be carrying the remains of eating and drinking plus wet and smelly clothes! Be prepared. See the Checklists. Putting the children in dark or highly patterned clothes will make the amount of dirt less visible!

KEEPING THE CHILDREN ENTERTAINED

Keeping a child contented on a long journey is an art. Although older children may well bury their heads in books you cannot rely on this, nor is it advisable for children to look down if they are prone to travel sickness in cars. There is a wide variety of modestly priced quiz, puzzle and activity books available. Keep a pack of surprises in your hand luggage in case of delays.

Food can be one of your best allies; maybe relax the rules about sweets, or provide apples, biscuits or tiny boxes of raisins. But don't take chocolate or chocolate biscuits, however popular, unless you want a really revolting mess on the back seat. The section on Travel Sickness outlines what foods to avoid when setting out on a journey.

If you are not going to annoy others you can sing songs, and cassettes are very useful. Personal stereo systems are marvellous when the train or plane is crowded. Some lending libraries have tapes or, if you are planning a very long journey, you could pick something interesting from the 'Tapeworm' catalogue which describes and prices over 100 cassettes for children. Older children like stories but even the youngest child will listen to nursery rhymes: we recommend Playgroup Songtime (Music for Pleasure) or the range of song tapes sold by the Early Learning Centre. Take a popular song book or, for pre-school children, a nursery rhyme book or *This Little Puffin*, compiled by Elizabeth Matterson.

Occupations could include:

Games   Magnetic ones like draughts and Chinese chequers; Travel Scrabble or wipe clean board games; a pack of cards.

Books   *I Spy* and *Observer* books. The AA sells a *Travel Games* book and books suitable for those over 6 called *Fun in Britain*, *Fun in France*, *Fun in Spain* and *Fun in Italy*. *Favourite Games for Your Journey* has endless games and quizzes for all age groups. The *Usborne Book of Travel Games* is good for over 10s. The *Piccolo Book of Travelling Games* includes many oldies and some new ones too.

Activities   For under 8s try something the child is not familiar with, such as a wipe clean magic slate or Magic Pictures, from Galt and others. Colouring books and crayons are essentials – try paint-sticks from the Early Learning Centre. Toddlers and babies can be entertained by balloons, bubbles and puppets on sticks. Are your children old enough to carry their own bag of amusements (maybe in a child's rucksack)?

DRIVING

If you are driving a lot in Europe, the *Travellers Guide to Europe* contains useful information country by country on speed restrictions, whether garages accept credit cards, international driving licences, and much more.

Travel schedule

It might suit you best to travel at night with the children asleep (if there's enough room), particularly on summer holiday weekends. Try to travel with another adult. Driving in a new area is not recommended without a navigator, especially if there is sarcasm from the back. If you have to make the journey alone, plan plenty of breaks.

Remember that storing half your gear on the roof rack will slow you down considerably as it affects stability. Check with the motoring organisations for speed restrictions if taking a trailer.

Safety

It's an indisputable fact that the safest place for a child to travel in a car is on the back seat properly restrained by an approved safety seat, harness or seat belt. If your children are not big enough to see out of the windows, they will appreciate booster seats.

When driving with young children, it is important to check that your childproof door safety locks work. Always use them.

If you are hiring a car, ask at the time of booking about child locks, child car seats and rear safety belts. Hertz offer to arrange car seats throughout Europe for a non-refundable charge, although they have to be returned to the office where they were hired. However, car seats seem to be in short supply with many companies on the Continent and pre-booking does not necessarily result in one being ready for you when you arrive. Travelling with unrestrained small children in the back seat may be a new experience for you and for them. They will probably fight and jump around in their new found freedom and you can't be sure whether that sudden movement in your rear view mirror was a child's arm or an overtaking motorbike. With small children an adult will have to sit in the rear as well, ready to clutch on to them every time you negotiate a hairpin bend.

Seat belts and the law

As a general rule it is recommended that children do not ride in the front seat, although this may help alleviate car sickness for some. In Britain no children can travel in the front seat of a car under 14 unless they are in an 'approved restraint' such as a *Babysafe* seat. Most European countries have restrictions on the ages of front seat passengers:

● No children under 12: Belgium, Eire, Norway, Portugal, Switzerland and Yugoslavia. Except when using special seats or safety belts suitable for children: Austria. Except children over 4 using a hip safety belt and under 4 using a safety seat of approved design: the Netherlands. Except for children under 4 in a reverse position seat: Sweden.

● No children under 10: Algeria, Andorra, France and Greece.

● No children under 8: Tunisia.

● Children under 12 not permitted where rear seating is available: West Germany.

● There are no restrictions in Denmark, Italy, Morocco or Spain.

Keeping the children entertained in cars

Make plans for entertainment if undertaking a long journey with under 10s, although, if you are lucky, your children will be rocked to sleep by the motion of the car for part of the journey. Motorway driving can be especially tedious, and there are many games you cannot play as there is relatively little for the children to see out of the windows. Make regular breaks, possibly at family orientated places such as L'Arche on the French autoroutes or Happy Eater in the UK where the kids can use the indoor and outdoor play equipment while you wait to be served.

Find a focus to your stops, such as a playground or a picnic, and drive slowly past sights which interest your children, like a herd of animals or a man on a donkey. Directories and guide books will help you plan your stops. *Kids' Britain* and *Off the Motorway* are excellent for Britain. As already mentioned veto reading and games which require the children to look down, especially if they are prone to car-sickness.

Travelling with a baby

In Britain and abroad, motorway service areas usually have mother and baby facilities (although you might find it more comfortable to breast-feed in the privacy of your car). It may be more hygienic to change the baby in the car or on the hatchback parcel shelf than in a garage lavatory. A small rug or blanket is useful for making your child cosy and as a picnic rug.

COACH TRAVEL

Your problems will be similar to those when travelling by car except that you will not have a child restraint, but with luck other people will help you in the amusement game.

FLYING

Interest your children in the forthcoming flight. Your child could make a model of the aircraft you will fly in, or a toddler might like a toy plane. Books on flying might be appreciated: we suggest *The Superbook of Aircraft*, for any age up to 10 and *If I were a Pilot* for the pre-school child.

At the time of booking

Advise the airline or operator that you will have children or babies with you. Travel light but with a spare jumper as the air conditioning can be cool and, on disembarking, summer evenings in warm climes can be surprisingly chilly.

At the airport

Check in early to have a choice of seat – near the window for viewing, near the aisle for easy access to the loo, or a bulkhead seat so that they can't climb over the head of the man in front. You can always fill in the time between check-in and flight by spotting planes. At Gatwick, for example, you can go to a viewing platform, for a small entrance charge; it is at the north end of the building and has its own coffee bar.

Most British and foreign airports offer good facilities for mothers with babies and toddlers. These are your havens, particularly in the case of a delay or a missed flight.

Baggage

Fare-paying children usually have an adult baggage allowance. The allowance for under 2s is confined to food for consumption on the flight, a carrying basket and nappies. (Emergency diapers are only carried on intercontinental flights.) Collapsible pushchairs and strollers, which are not generally counted as part of the baggage allowance, may be permitted in the passenger cabin but are normally put in the aircraft hold at the last minute. Don't check yours in with your suitcases; airport corridors can be long.

Take-off and landing

See the section on Health for advice on avoiding ear discomfort.

Keeping the children entertained

Personal stereo systems are permitted on aeroplanes but only when the seatbelt sign is not lit. A new story tape might fill part of that four-hour journey to Crete, and the in-flight magazine may include some games. The airlines try to arrange for visits to the flight deck provided the captain is not too busy.

Food and drink

Usually the food is not suitable for fussy eaters or babies and toddlers. Balancing the loaded tray on your lap together with the baby and trying to open little plastic packets with your teeth for your older child does not make for happy eating. Even drinking is difficult. If the fruit juice runs

out, you will be left with the option of spicy tomato or fizzy soda. Flight attendants will only warm and cool bottles. (Emergency baby food is available only on intercontinental flights.) You should buy food in jars for the plane and take at least one more bottle than you think you will need in case of delays. If you are breast-feeding, take a plastic bottle of water to drink. Long flights mean dehydration and, on a more mundane level, fewer visits to the loo.

Changing facilities

There are normally no facilities for changing nappies, although some loos have changing tables (wide-bodied 747s and DC10 airliners, for example). You will have to use the floor.

TRAINS

This is one of the best ways to travel with your family. The children can read, draw or write and, if necessary, move around.

Although there is a charge of £1 per seat, it may be sensible to reserve them in advance. Try to travel midweek and not at peak times. Buy your tickets in advance, either from the station or a travel agent, so that you can go directly to the platform on arrival at the station.

You do not have long to lift children, luggage, pushchairs and so forth into the carriage, unless you are joining the train at a terminus. If you are

travelling on your own with the children, ask for help getting on and off, and if you need to change platforms approach the nearest person in rail uniform for assistance (maybe you can use the mail lift rather than staircases). Why not carry your gear in a rucksask or the baby in a backpack, to keep your hands free? Try to find a carriage near the buffet car if you need bottles to be warmed, drinks or food. If you are travelling with little ones, there are usually no facilities. The new image British Rail might like to note that some French trains have fully equipped play areas for children, with seating opposite for parents. They also have nurseries where the babies can be changed and fed, not to mention non-stop discotheque bars for teenagers.

FERRIES

Travelling by ferry is an exciting start to the holiday. One family who travelled from Harwich to Esbjerg said their 'mini-cruise' was the most successful way that they had ever journeyed out of this country, and other families have commented on how exciting their children had found 'the ship'. But bear in mind that besides being breezy up on deck the lounges may be air-conditioned, so take warm clothing. Confirm that blankets and pillows are provided on night crossings.

At the ferry terminal

Although you need to check in on time, try not to be too early or you will have a boring, cramped wait in your car. Departure lounges rarely have enough seats, food is uninspiring and it's easy to lose track of the children in the crowds. Early arrival does not ensure good seats.

Seats and cabins

You could consider booking reclining seats if travelling by day on a long crossing. Make sure the seats are beside one another, not just consecutive numbers.

If your children are very young, think about booking a day cabin (do not count on getting one once you are on board, as only a few are staffed during the day). When you book, say that you have a small child and must be on the top deck of the cabins; lower deck stairways are very steep and it can be a long way to the main promenade. The £12 or so charge can allow the family to rest, play and picnic in privacy, while baby can be fed and changed in comfort and you are not burdened with hand luggage wherever you go. If you hope to use a travel cot, check that it will fit into the cabin (they are fine in all four-berthers).

Sea sickness

See the section on Keeping Healthy on Holiday for hints on how to avoid sickness.

Food

All cross-Channel and North Sea ferries sell food and most serve children's portions. However, the food can be expensive or uninspiring, the cafeteria may be closed or have a very long queue, so consider taking a picnic for the children. Adults might prefer to wait until they reach France!

High chairs are normally provided in the waiter service restaurant, but the number and quality vary. In high season you have to get into the restaurant very early to get a baby chair at all.

Keeping the children entertained

On some ferries there may be entertainment for children, usually in the form of a video lounge. Facilities vary from boat to boat even within one company: at worst there will be a playroom with no toys and at best they can be like the DFDS ferry *Tor Scandinavia* with children's cartoons, treasure hunts, drawing competitions, an interesting playroom and a sheltered, heated swimming pool, or the Olau ferries with playrooms (housing a slide and Lego sets) and an indoor swimming pool.

Changing facilities

Most ships have a mother and baby area in one of the ladies' loos, with a kitchen of sorts if you are lucky, a changing mat and curtained off feeding chair.

Keeping Healthy on Holiday

You will all want to keep in the best of health on holiday to enjoy it to the full. Although you may not be able to avoid appendicitis or even a cold, a little bit of forethought and care can make the difference between your holiday being a success or a disaster.

If you are fussy about your family's health, why not send £1 for the British Medical Association's *Health on Holiday* booklet or borrow one of the many publications on healthy holidays from the library? These should answer all your queries. But if this still isn't enough, you could always try the computerised service available from the Medical Advisory Services for Travellers Abroad. They will send details of required vaccinations and preventative drugs, health do's and don'ts and what medical items to pack. The Brief Guide (immunisation and malaria only) costs £4.75. The Concise Edition for holidays costs £9.50, while a Comprehensive Guide is £25. Application forms are available from chemists and from MASTA, Keppel St, London WC1E 7HT (01-631 4408).

Think through your family's health care needs and consider the following well before departure.

ADVANCE PREPARATION

Present health   If you are concerned about some aspect of your health or your children's health, consult your doctor, dentist or health visitor before you leave. Finding a doctor or dentist on holiday can be time-consuming and expensive.

Current medication   Take with you all the medicine that you think you may need plus half as much again. You may not be able to find the formula you are used to, even in remote parts of Britain, and overseas it will almost certainly be expensive. Ask your doctor to write down the pharmacological names of any regular medication and take a note of when and how much should be taken. Ensure you know the proper name of any substance to which your family is sensitive or allergic.

Spectacles   If any member of your family wears glasses, take a spare pair.

Vaccinations   Check vaccination requirements. There are usually none for anyone travelling to Europe; nevertheless ensure that your children are up to date with their routine jabs. If you are travelling outside

Europe, North America or Australia, there may be a requirement for vaccinations against polio, typhoid, tetanus, yellow fever, cholera or infectious hepatitis, although pregnant women and those under a year may be exempt. The latest recommendations are set out in the DHSS leaflet, *Protect Your Health Abroad*, available from travel agents and social security offices, or you can contact Thomas Cook's Medical Centre for advice. It is best to organise vaccinations well in advance as some take weeks to be effective. However, a late visit to your doctor or the medical centre at Heathrow or Gatwick is better than nothing. If you are travelling to a malarious area (parts of Turkey are affected), you will need to take prophylactic drugs before, during and after the holiday. These are not recommended for babies under 3 months or for expectant mothers.

Pregnant women   Restrictions on flying when pregnant start at about 26 weeks, though most airlines will permit you to travel up to 32 weeks on short hauls. After this time you may need a doctor's certificate stating that you are fit to travel. Check with the airline. This is not so much because high pressure in the plane is likely to induce labour but because of the enormous problems posed for cabin staff, who are not trained to cope on a cramped and crowded flight, and the tremendous expense involved if the flight has to be rerouted to get you to hospital. On a short haul, you are more likely to have the baby in the airport terminal than on the plane. Also make sure your insurance policy does not exclude complications arising from pregnancy.

A MEDICAL KIT

This should be packed near the top of your luggage where it will be easily accessible. 'Just as we piled into our car after our overnight stop, Edward, determined not to be left behind, fell down the steps to the road and grazed his knees badly. And where was the first aid kit? Right at the bottom of our bulging and carefully packed boot!'

Boots sell a ready-made Holiday Kit with a health guide at around £6. However, it does not contain medicines because of the danger of breakage and the shelf life of the product. You can also make up your own. You will know what you want to include, depending on the ages of your children, where you are going and what sort of activities you are planning. We recommend the following:

● Analgesics for headaches and other pains

● Sun barrier creams and something to soothe sunburn

- An insect repellent and bite and sting remedies
- Travel sickness remedy
- Sticking plasters
- Antiseptic cream and wipes
- Rehydration sachets

You might also consider

- An indigestion remedy
- Anti-diarrhoea mixture
- Thermometer (instruments containing mercury are not allowed on planes so try a liquid crystal one or disposables)
- Water sterilising tablets
- Eye wash (to relieve soreness caused by sun and salt)

You can also buy a homoeopathic First Aid kit from homoeopathic stockists or from Nelson's Mail Order which costs £15. This together with a travel sickness remedy would be an adequate holiday kit.

THE JOURNEY

Travel sickness

The warning signs are yawning, salivation, cold sweating and dizziness. Sickness can be aggravated by over-excitement or fear of the journey. Some children may be car-sick on the way there but never on the way back. Other factors which can contribute are smells and sights, such as others being sick, or over-indulging before starting the journey. It seems more prevalent if there is a family history of asthma, migraine, eczema or hayfever.

To help your child:

- Avoid fried or greasy foods before the journey. Keep meals light and simple with no dairy produce and chocolate. Any fruit, except the citrus varieties, is fine. Give pure juice to drink (not citric) or, best of all, plain water.

- For car-sickness try and keep attention focused on the horizon. Seat the children, if possible, so that they have a clear view ahead. If you don't often sit in the back, you probably don't realise how much vision is blocked by headrests in the front and how easily you can remove them. Try to dissuade the children from looking out of the side and rear windows, and ask the driver to corner slowly. Rear seat belts help to stop the rolling about not noticed in front seats. Older children might be better off in the front passenger seat, if permitted.

● Never give reading material or a game which necessitates looking down to children prone to sickness.

● Place the carrycot or little seat for a small child in the smoothest part of the car, train, coach, boat or hovercraft and try to plan to travel during nap time.

● Ensure good ventilation. Take the children up on deck in a boat or open a window in a car.

If you spot warning signs, break the journey if possible and allow the child to walk around for a few minutes. Sucking barley sugar, nibbling plain biscuits or eating something containing ginger have also been found helpful. If you think your child is still likely to be sick then you can try a travel sickness remedy. The following can be purchased at most chemists:

Phenergen syrup useful for small children who hate to take tablets.

Sea Legs suitable for 2 years old and over. They can be chewed or taken with water.

Joy Rides for 3 years old and over. The tablets are chewable and flavoured.

Kwells for over 4s, also chewable, flavoured tablets.

There are also homoeopathic travel sickness tablets which are especially suited to small children as no drugs are involved.

If your child is likely to be sick when in the car, you could do worse than hide a used ice cream tub under the front seat, complete with toilet roll and baby wipes. The smell can then be shut in the box until you reach a lavatory. A damp cloth sprinkled with bicarbonate of soda will take away the smell of any splashes on the seats and floor. If your child is always being sick, put newspapers across the back seat and take protective clothing or spare outfits.

Air travel

Children can be given a boiled sweet to suck, while babies should suck from the breast or bottle. As there may be pain in the ears due to changes in atmospheric pressure during take-off and landing, children should be instructed to pinch their noses and blow, so creating internal pressure in the ears to counteract the external changes. Swallowing and yawning also help.

Ask your doctor for a gentle sedative for your toddler if you are going on a long night flight and are worried that he or she may be up and about when the rest of the passengers are bedded down.

WHEN YOU ARRIVE

Food and Water

In a strange place there may be bacteria to which you are unused and which can produce an attack of diarrhoea lasting 24–48 hours. If you are holidaying in any area where you suspect the water is not safe, then it should be sterilised, not only for drinking but also for washing salads and fruit and for cleaning teeth. You may also find that the local water tastes foul. Your alternatives are:

● Boiling for at least five minutes. This is the best way to sterilise drinking water, but you will then have to wait for it to cool! A Pifco Mini Boiler can be bought from electrical outlets.

● Bottled water. Choose a still one without a high mineral content which could cause diarrhoea in children. Watch in restaurants to make sure the seal on the bottle is not broken, otherwise it could be bottled tap water.

● Sterilising tablets can also be used. Read the instructions carefully and remember that the solution will have to stand for some time. As children may find the chlorine taste unpleasant, you may need to add something for flavour.

Be wary of food purchased from stalls, shops, or cafés that hasn't been well screened or refrigerated. Shellfish can be particularly hazardous. Ice may not be safe if it has been made with unsterilised water.

Ice cream is a classic problem as it may have been allowed to part melt and then refrozen and may contain salmonella bacteria. Avoid that battered old freezer in the back of the café at the end of the season and look for fast moving fresh stock.

Keep reminding everybody to wash their hands after using strange lavatories. Babies pick up gastro-intestinal infections more easily than adults and need special care. It is wise to delay weaning until after the holiday.

Don't panic if a child who is not obviously ill develops diarrhoea, but if it continues for three days see a doctor.

If the child has stomach pains, is feverish and is vomiting, you should consult a doctor without delay. Babies under one year lose fluids so quickly from an attack of diarrhoea that they can be in serious danger. Call a doctor and give as much liquid as possible whilst waiting. If the attack is very severe, you should use rehydration sachets, such as *Dioralyte*, to be diluted with sterilised water to counteract dehydration. A home-made, but less pleasant tasting substitute is a solution of half a teaspoon of salt and four teaspoons of sugar in a litre of sterilised water.

Sunburn

Sunburn can be very serious for children, in extreme cases leading to hospitalisation even in Britain. The first rule is avoidance; even an adult should not be out for more than half an hour on the first day of a Mediterranean holiday. You can gradually lengthen exposure as the holiday progresses, but always try to keep small children out of the midday sun. It is also possible to burn badly on hazy days when the sun is overcast, especially when there is a strong breeze blowing. Ultra violet rays are also reflected from buildings, sand, water and snow.

The second rule is protection. Ensure that children wear hats and long sleeved tops, particularly the baby who should not be directly exposed to the sun. Sunshades on buggies are often thin and small, ineffective if you are walking and turning in different directions. You should consider lining yours or adding another layer (e.g. a cardigan draped over the top) in strong sun. Fair-skinned and red-headed children are more likely to burn.

The sunscreen you choose should screen out the ultra violet A rays as well as the B rays and it's best to opt for a high sun protection factor (these give you a guide to the amount of time one can safely stay in the sun and range from 2 to 15). Use a total sunblock for sensitive areas like lips, ears and eyelids and burned parts which need protection. Water resistant sunscreens are best for the pool or beach and should be reapplied every few hours.

If children do get sunburnt, they should stay inside. They can get sunburnt even under an umbrella. Cold baths or showers (but without the soap as this can irritate) will help soothe the pain. Then apply a cooling lotion such as calamine or one of the many aftersun products.

Heat exhaustion is serious and is due to water or salt deprivation. Fainting from heat is a well-known symptom, but others will develop headaches and nausea while the temperature remains normal. An unwell child should be put to bed, preferably in a cool room, with the head in a low position. You should administer fluids with added salt to prevent the development of heatstroke or sunstroke.

Some children also suffer from prickly heat – a rash caused when the sweat cannot escape through the ducts and evaporate. You can prevent this by ensuring the child wears loose cotton clothes and avoids too much exercise and exposure to excessive moist heat. There are special talcum powders available in some countries.

Dehydration

In hot weather children can suffer dehydration and salt loss. To prevent this, particularly in the car, ensure that ventilation is adequate and that the sun is not beating down on them. Loose, light clothing is best. Requests for drinks should be satisfied. Babies in carrycots should be tucked in as lightly as possible commensurate with their safety.

You can add a level teaspoon of salt to 1.1 litres (2 pints) of drink to counteract salt loss from perspiration in very hot weather.

Bites and stings

Gnats, midges and mosquitoes are most numerous near fresh water. Mosquitoes generally attack in the evening or after dark. You will not only encounter them abroad: Scottish midges are infamous. Put your child in long-sleeved tops with long-legged trousers or long-sleeved/long-legged pyjamas to ensure peaceful nights. You can use a swatter or spray-repellent in the bedroom with as many doors and windows closed as good ventilation will allow. You can also use a little electric machine which burns tablets, or burn a coil (both available in shops in mosquito infested areas). If bitten, ice or a cooling spray, with calamine, will provide some relief. If your child has not been exposed to mosquitoes before, it may take a couple of weeks to develop an intolerance.

Bee and wasp stings   Bees leave the shaft of the sting in the skin and it is important to scratch it out immediately with a fingernail. Relief can be obtained with sodium bicarbonate paste and by applying ice, cold compresses or a cooling lotion or spray. Vinegar will provide relief from wasp stings plus cold applications of a product such as *Waspeeze*.

Jellyfish may be a problem. Ask local advice about swimming. If your child is stung, rub the area with handfuls of wet sand and try to remove the tentacles and give relief by applying alcohol and cooling lotions.

Sea urchins and other spiny sea creatures may cause unpleasant skin punctures. The best immediate remedy is urine. Lemon juice will do for the more fastidious. Treat the wounds with an antiseptic cream.

Animals abroad Don't let your children play with or stroke them as even those appearing docile and friendly may be suffering from rabies. If a bite or scratch does happen, wash the wound at once with detergent or soap and try to find out whether the animal has been vaccinated (ask to see the certificate). If not, rush to the doctor.

Illness on holiday

If you are worried about your child's health at any time, give plenty to drink and discourage eating. If he or she does fall ill and you are in a country where you do not speak the language, we think it is worth travelling a little further to see an English-speaking doctor. You may still have difficulty in understanding or in being understood. If you are on a package tour ask the courier to accompany you as it is almost certainly part of the job to do so. Suppositories and injections are common ways of giving medicines on the Continent so ask the doctor specifically for oral medicine as your child is bound to prefer this.

Holidaying With a Baby or Toddler

All the families we have talked to stress the need for careful planning and ample supplies of food, drinks, clothing and nappies.

When to go?

If your baby is entirely breast-fed, life will be easiest if you go before you start solid feeding. If you are bottle-feeding the opposite is true, unless you are self-catering and the journey is fairly short. It is most difficult to go in the period when baby is taking solids but not eating finger food, and you are still sterilising equipment. Of course if you wait until this period is over you have nearly reached the stage where the baby is crawling around and getting into everything!

Bear in mind that difficulties over going to sleep often start around 9 months and that a disturbance to routine like going away on holiday might be better avoided at this time.

Don't let us put you off having a holiday entirely – at least babies are fairly easily transported and you can enjoy the last vestiges of life as it used to be. You'll be surprised by the number of people who will say, 'Gosh, you are brave,' which will make you feel wonderful.

Cots

The one supplied may not be as smart as yours at home! The mattress may not have a waterproof cover and you can imagine the condition it might be in. If you consider the cot is dangerous, but it is not possible to have it changed, try to modify it by wrapping towels round the bars, etc. Check the following:

● The construction should be secure: there should be no loose screws and no holes in the wire mesh base.

● There should be no dangerous fittings such as wooden or metal knobs, or loose screws, which might catch clothing or bedding.

● Any peeling paint or pictures inside the cot should be removed completely.

● The depth of the cot, without mattress, should be at least 26 in (65 cm) to stop the baby climbing out. Any gap between the mattress base and bottom rail should be no more than 1 in (2.5 cm).

● Bars should be plain and parallel to prevent the baby's hand, foot or head getting trapped.

● The mattress should fit snugly within the frame to protect the baby from the wire mesh underneath and be deep enough to prevent the baby slipping out.

Clothes

You will not need to pack so much if you are going south in sunny weather, as summer things can be washed and dried quickly. If you are staying in northern Europe or going away in winter and have space in your luggage, consider borrowing cast-off clothes from friends' children to alleviate the chore of washing and drying. If you are going skiing, remember that hotels and chalets are heated to unbelievable temperatures, so take T-shirts and thin clothing for indoors.

Food

Even if you do not normally use jars of babyfood, you will find them easier to manage when travelling than tins or packets. Should your baby dislike cold food, travel with a wide-necked vacuum flask to reheat by immersion. You can buy tins of baby milk, jars (e.g. Gerber) and packets of babyfood all over Europe and the USA; but if your baby is wedded to a brand, such as Wy-Soy, or you are concerned about sugar- and gluten-free products, then buy a generous supply for the whole holiday. On the Continent you will find some of the jars of babyfood quite exotic: squid with tomatoes or globe artichoke with potatoes, for example. Take enough food to allow for delays on the journey or to avoid rising at dawn in a strange place to look for a shop.

Milk

If your bottle-fed baby is under 6 months you will need to take a kit to prepare bottles. Mix a locally-bought modified milk powder with sterilised water (see the section on Keeping Healthy on Holiday) heated up, if necessary, with a Pifco Mini Boiler or similar in a pyrex jug. Serve in a Playtex container into which you insert a sterilised plastic bag from a roll. Thus, feeding equipment is reduced to a bottle, two teats, the plastic bags, sterilising tablets and a screw topped jar with a plastic lid. We are told that empty Sainsbury's large-sized polythene parmesan tubs fit the bill for the last nicely.

Older babies can drink local milk as long as it is pasteurised, or UHT, or tinned evaporated milk diluted 3:1. If you are breast-feeding you will find it easiest to delay weaning until after the holiday. A small insulated bag, such as the kind sold for children to use for packed lunches or picnics, is just right for holding two prepared bottles and an ice pack for your journey. Again don't forget to take more than enough for the journey.

Nappies

Warm weather means that children eat less and drink more. They also urinate less. If they suit your child, use disposables which are easier for holidays than towelling nappies. All-in-one disposables are widely available in Europe and the USA so you need pack only sufficient for the journey plus a few days' supply. In some places they may be unavailable or surprisingly expensive: we had one report of a baby with diarrhoea in St Lucia where each nappy cost 50 pence.

If you have not used disposables before, try them out before you go. In a hot climate muslin nappies could be more comfortable and will dry quickly. Baby wipes, nappy rash ointment, and, if you must use towelling nappies, Napisan and nappy liners may be difficult to obtain.

Entertainment

Your child will not need many toys as everything will be interesting in the new environment. Keep something aside for the tedious part of the journey when your offspring will be confined in a small space. If you expect bad weather you will need more toys than if going to the sun. A favourite cuddly animal plus a new version of an old well-used toy is a good combination, but keep an eye on the beloved animal – you don't want it dropped and lost just as you are about to board the plane. You might like to think about taking something new as this could be the time to learn to master a new skill.

Equipment tips

You will certainly not need every item in the following list. There is definitely no need to buy new equipment: secondhand shops, small ads and hiring (many NCT groups have travel cots to rent) are all valuable ways of collecting together what you need. Your most important sources, however, will be those friends who are willing to lend and swap. Borrowing, for example, a sunshade for the buggy or swapping your ordinary buggy for a friend's lie-back can be very helpful.

High chairs   If you have a baby aged 0–9 months you may be able to improvise with a sling (if you have one). If you are taking a baby bouncing chair you can use this, or you may have a *Loveseat* or similar car seat (next paragraph). For those aged 6–18 months you could use a Britax car seat with a tray, which can be removed easily from the car and will double as a high chair. Mothercare, Maclaren and Cindico sell a tray which clips on to some of their buggies. Otherwise there are cloth restrainers like *Tamsit* and the *Easy Seat Chair Harness* from Easy Rider which tie the baby into most dining chairs. Mothercare's foldaway table seat can be attached to any table. Similar models are *The Baby Diner* chair from Kiddy Mail and the *Sassy Seat* by Emcorp Ltd. If you own a Mothercare *Supersitter*, *Baby Relax* from Boots or similar, then you can travel with just the little chair and tray and place it on the floor. If all else fails, try to fit your fold-up high chair into your car boot. For toddlers, the Mothercare *Sit-at-Table* seat, the Boots *Top Seat* or the *Seat Raiser*, available from Kiddy Mail, would be invaluable; they raise a child on an ordinary chair to table height and will be useful at home afterwards when you abandon the high chair.

Car seats   For babies 0–9 months, or under 22 lb (10 kg) consider using a reverse facing baby seat – the *Babysafe* from Britax, the *Loveseat* or Mothercare's similar model which you can strap, using adult seat belts, into the front or the rear. It won't take up as much room as a carrycot and is said to be safer. On a hot day your baby will be more comfortable travelling in just a nappy with no stifling carrycot cover.

Somewhere to sleep   Jillymac produce a shoulder bag which when unzipped becomes a carrycot suitable for small babies, but it is not robust enough to strap into the car. Babies may sleep better in their own travel cot than that provided at your destination. Choose a travel cot which is large enough and has high enough sides for an active child who is already beginning to climb, and get a pernickety baby used to the travel cot before departure. Mothercare sell a *Junior Travel Bed* which has a fixed cover for pre-school children.

Pushchairs   Light weight, compact and easily collapsible buggies are essential. A lie-back is recommended so that the baby can snooze better while you are at a restaurant or travelling in a train.

Slings These are a useful alternative to a pram or pushchair. You can use a sling from birth but until about 10 weeks you will have to make sure that the baby's head is supported.

Back-packs For heavier babies try one of these frame seats which hook over the shoulders like a rucksack. If you are planning long walks the secret of success is to practise using it before your holiday. If you are often on your own with the baby you will need to be able to put it on and to adjust the straps without help. There are various makes such as Karrimor or the Cindico *Bak-Sac*. The *Serenade Baby Carrier* is the model for serious walkers and it folds down small enough for suitcases, whereas the Cindico and Mothercare models fold to only 9 in (22 cm) deep.

Changing mats Why not buy a piece of PVC off a roll? You can also put it under the high chair or use it as a waterproof sheet to save the embarrassment of spoiling your relatives' bedding. Otherwise, use your changing bag, if you have one.

Potties You can buy a lid for some potties, e.g. Boots. There are even inflatable potties, the *Bubble Potty* available from Kiddy Mail, with disposable liners.

Baby baths If you really need one, you could invest in an inflatable plastic bath. Most self-catering accommodation has a washing-up bowl or sink large enough to bath a small baby. If your accommodation is only provided with a shower, take a rubber plug with a universal fitting

(available from good ironmongers) so that you can bathe your reluctant toddler in three inches of water in the shower tray if necessary.

Trainer mugs   The Avent feeding system (from Boots) has a 9 oz (250 ml) bottle with a wide neck which will take teats or a screw on, leak-proof travel lid or a trainer top. There are also jars for carrying food. The *Early Days* beaker has a spill-proof seal. You can interchange a trainer top with a teat top on Maws bottles – just screw on a disc with a collar if you want to travel with them full. Otherwise travel with your trainer mug empty or put cling film under the lid to stop leaks.

Food heaters   If your baby is drinking milk, does it really have to be warmed? Maybe cold food would be appreciated just as well. If you must take an electric heater, then Mothercare sell one which can be plugged into the car cigarette lighter.

Bibs   Find a softish plastic one to eliminate washing, or a plastic apron if your baby does not take to Pelican bibs. Disposable ones are available from Mothercare and through Kiddy Mail.

Night lights   Battery operated ones are the most practical. Alternatively, improvise with a 15 watt bulb bought at your destination.

Checklists

We have made these lists as comprehensive as possible so you may not need all the items. Improvisation is the secret to travelling light – see the Equipment Tips. You will find it useful to make up your own list and to check it off as you pack. Keep it for the next holiday. Pack everything your family will need for the journey in one bag, and have it readily accessible in your hand luggage.

FOR YOUR JOURNEY

For babies under 1 year

- Bottle feeds
- Food in jars, a spoon and rusks
- Bib
- Disposable nappies
- Changing mat
- J cloth in a plastic bag or individual baby wipes
- Tissues or toilet roll
- Plastic bags
- Complete change of clothes
- A jumper
- Sling, babyseat or carrycot
- Buggy or framed back pack
- Dummy or comforter

For toddlers

In addition to the items for babies, consider:

- Beaker
- Spoon
- Drink
- Snack
- Nappy changing kit or spare pants
- Harness and reins
- Toys and books

FOR YOUR DESTINATION

For babies under 1 year

In addition to clothing take:

- Bottle-feeding equipment
- Food
- Vitamin drops
- Baby lotion
- Shampoo
- Barrier cream
- Cotton wool
- Nappies and paraphernalia
- Nappy pins or tape for unfamiliar nappies
- Extra J cloths
- Rainhood for buggy
- Wet weather gear
- Sunshade or sun umbrella for buggy
- Travel cot or carrycot
- Bedding
- Insect net for cot
- Improvised high chair
- Swimming pants
- Arm bands
- Hat
- Suncream

For toddlers

You may also need:

- Waterproof bedsheet
- Improvised night light
- Sand shoes
- Bucket and spade
- Wellingtons and clothing for wet weather
- Duvet and cover – their own one
- Potty or little seat
- Washing and teeth-cleaning kit
- Safety protectors – a stair gate, elastic bands and string, masking tape

Appendix 1. Books and Guides

Prices are for 1986 guides

AA Camping and Caravanning in Britain; pub AA; £4.95.
AA Camping and Caravanning in Europe; pub AA; £5.95.
Activity and Hobby Holidays, England; English Tourist Board; £1.99.
Activity Holidays in Britain & the Channel Islands; pub FHG; 75p.
Adventure Holidays; Simon Calder, pub Vacation-Work; £3.95.
Cade's Self-catering Holiday Guide; pub Cade's; £1.10.
Camping in Comfort; Dymphna Byrne; pub Hamlyn; £1.75.
Camping Sites in Britain; pub Link House; £1.75.
Capital Guide for Kids; Vanessa Miles; pub Allison & Busby; £1.95.
Caravan and Camp Sites in Britain; Ed, Frederick Tingey; pub Letts Guides;
   £2.75.
Children's London; London Tourist Board; 60p.
Children's Guide to London; Christopher Pick; Cadogan Books; £3.95.
Children Welcome; A Herald Holiday Handbook; pub FHG; 95p.
Discovering London for Children; Margaret Pearson; Shire Publications; £1.75.
England's Seaside; English Tourist Board; £1.95.
Family Welcome Guide; Jill Foster and Malcolm Hamer; pub Sphere; £4.95.
Farm & Country Holidays in England, Wales and Scotland; Pastime Publications;
   95p.
Farm Holiday Guide, England; pub FHG; £1.25. (Also guides for *Wales and
   Ireland* together and for *Scotland*).
Farm Holidays in Britain; pub Farm Holiday Bureau in association with the
   English Tourist Board; £1.95.
Favourite Games for Your Journey; Jane Cable-Alexander; pub Bell & Hyman;
   99p.
French Farm and Village Holiday Guide; pub McCarta Ltd, £4.75.
Fun in Britain. Also separate books for *France*, *Spain* and *Italy*; pub AA; £1.50.
Good Camps Guide for Britain; Alan Rogers; pub Deneway Guides and Travel;
   £1.50.
Good Holiday Cottage Guide; pub Swallow Press; £1.95.
Guesthouses, Farmhouses and Inns in Britain; pub AA; £4.95.
Guesthouses, Farmhouses and Inns in Europe; pub AA; £3.95.
Holidays and Travel Abroad: a Guide for Disabled People; Ed, D. McGhie; pub
   Royal Association for Disability and Rehabilitation; £1.00.
Holidays for Disabled People; pub Royal Association for Disability and Rehabili-
   tation; £2.00.
Holiday Homes, Cottages and Apartments in Britain; pub AA; £4.95.
If I were a Pilot; David Bennett; pub Sainsbury's/Walker Books; 95p.

Illustrated Guide to Britain's Coast; pub AA Publications/Hodder and Stoughton; £14.95.

Inland Waterway Guide; pub Brittan Publications/Inland Waterways Association; 95p.

I-Spy – Cars, Car Numbers, Civil Aircraft, On a Train Journey, At the Airport etc.; pub I-Spy; 65p.

International Youth Hostel Handbook, Volume 1, *Europe*; pub International Federation of Youth Hostels; £2.95.

Jonathan Lewis's Family Holiday Guide; Lewis Publications; 95p.

Kids' Britain; Betty Jerman; pub Pan Books; £2.95.

Kids' London; Elizabeth Holt and Molly Perham; pub Piccolo; £2.50.

Lazy Man's Guide to Holidays Afloat; pub Boat Enquiries; 95p.

Mini-Break Holidays in Britain; A Herald Holiday Handbook; pub FHG; 50p.

Observer Books; pub Warne; £1.95–£2.95.

Off the Motorway; Christopher Pick; pub Cadogan Books; £3.95.

Practical Camper Sites; pub Haymarket; £1.75.

Piccolo Book of Travelling Games; Deborah Manley and Peta Ree; pub Pan Books; £1.95.

RAC Camping and Caravanning Campsite Guide – Europe; pub RAC; £3.95.

RAC Camping and Caravanning Campsite Guide – GB and Ireland; pub RAC; £2.50.

Scotland, Where to Stay, Hotels and Guesthouses; pub Scottish Tourist Board; £2.95.

Scottish Youth Hostels Association Handbook; pub Scottish YHA; 60p.

Spur Book of Family Camping; Pond; pub Spurbooks; £3.50.

Superbook of Aircraft; David Roberts; Kingfisher Books; £1.95.

This Little Puffin . . . Finger Plays and Nursery Games; compiled Elizabeth Matterson; Penguin Books; £1.75.

Travel Games; pub AA; £1.75.

Travellers' Guide for the Disabled; pub AA; £2.25.

Traveller's Guide to Europe; pub AA; £6.95.

Usborne Book of Travel Games; Tony Potter; Usborne Publishing; £2.95.

Where to Stay, England, Hotels; pub English Tourist Board; £3.95.

Where to Stay in London; pub London Convention and Visitor Bureau; £1.50.

YHA Guide; pub Youth Hostels Association; £1.50.

Appendix 2. Travel Companies and Useful Organisations

Most of the major tour companies' holidays can be booked through any travel agent. If you want to travel with Thomsons, Intasun, OSL, etc., simply go into your local travel agent and pick up a brochure. However, some of the operators mentioned in this book do not have brochures which you can collect quite so easily. These are:

The direct sales general tour companies set up in order to give the consumer a better deal by avoiding the travel agent's commission. The largest are Tjaereborg, Martin Rooks (a subsidiary of British Airways) and Portland (part of the Thomson group).

The direct sales specialists who offer a small, individual programme. They thrive on the personal contact with their clients and you gain from the individual attention you receive, although you will not generally gain the financial benefit from massive buying power for hotel rooms and plane seats. These companies are often used if you want to rent a cottage or gîte, go skiing or undertake a minority interest activity holiday.

Travel agents' own tours which can only be booked through that agent. These are either organised by a subsidiary company (e.g. Thomas Cook Holidays which are only available through Thomas Cook Travel Agents or Frames) or if the agent has negotiated an exclusive right to market on behalf of a tour company (e.g. W H Smith market Inn-Tent). If you do not live close to a branch of these travel agents, you can book by phone.

Brochures for all the holidays mentioned in this book can be obtained by contacting the companies at the addresses listed below. Where more than one enquiry address or telephone number is available, the London one has been given. The direct sales companies are indicated by **.

**AA,
See Automobile Association.

**ABTA,
55/57 Newman St,
London,
W1P 4AH.
01-637 2444

**Aegean Turkish Holidays,
10 South Molton St,
London,
W1Y 1DF.
01-499 9641
Pages 65, 80

Airtours,
Helmshore,
Rossendale,
Lancs,
BB4 4NB.
0706 21033
Page 65

**Allnatt Activity Holidays,
17 Knyveton Rd,
Bournemouth,
BH1 3QG.
0202 294799
Page 123

Ardmore Adventure,
23 Ramillies Place,
London,
W1V 1DG.
01-439 4461
Page 123

Arrow Holidays,
Alban Row,
27-31 Verulam Rd,
St Albans,
Herts,
AL3 4DG.
0727 6620011
Pages 66, 127

Arrowsmith Holidays,
Royal Buildings,
2 Mosley St,
Piccadilly,
Manchester,
M2 3AB.
061-236 1133
Pages 65, 66, 78, 80, 127

Aspro Holidays,
42 Bute St,
Cardiff,
CF1 5EW.
0222 481721
Pages 78, 80

**Automobile
    Association,
Fanum House,
Basingstoke,
Hants,
RG21 2EA.
0256 20123
Page 86

B & I Line Tours,
East Princes Dock,
Liverpool,
L3 0AA.
01-734 4861
Pages 34, 40, 55, 107

**B.U.A.C.
See British Universities
    Accommodation
    Consortium.

Balkan Holidays,
Sofia House,
19 Conduit St,
London,
W1R 9TD.
01-493 8612
Pages 66, 78

**Beach Villas,
8 Market Passage,
Cambridge,
CB2 3QR.
0223 311113
Pages 23, 65, 66, 70, 127

Belgian Travel Service,
Bridge House,
Ware,
Herts,
SG12 9DG.
0920 61131
Page 70

Best Holidays,
31 Topsfield Parade,
Crouch End,
London,
N8 8PT.
01-348 8211
Pages 78, 116

Bladon Lines,
56/58 Putney High St,
London,
SW15 1SF.
01-785 2200
Page 116

Blakes,
Wroxham,
Norwich,
NR12 8DH.
06053 3226
Pages 40, 60, 102, 130

Blue Sky Holidays,
Travel House,
Broxbourne,
Herts,
EN10 7JD.
0992 87299
Pages 24, 65, 66, 78, 80, 116

**Bowhill Cottages,
Mayhill Farm,
Swanmore,
Southampton,
SO3 2QW.
0489 877627
Page 70

**British Activity Holiday
    Association,
PO Box 99,
Tunbridge Wells,
Kent,
TN1 2EL.
0892 49868
Page 121

**British Horse Society,
BEC,
Stoneleigh,
Kenilworth,
Warwicks,
CV8 2LR.
0203 52241
Page 99

**British Medical
    Association,
BMA House,
Tavistock Square,
London,
WC1A 9JP.
01-387 4499
Page 151

**British Universities
    Accommodation
    Consortium,
PO Box F85,
University Park,
Nottingham,
NG7 2RD.
0602 504571
Pages 40, 59

**Brittany Ferries,
The Brittany Centre,
Wharf Rd,
Portsmouth,
PO2 8RU.
0705 827701
Pages 34, 70, 92

**Brittany Villas,
103a High St,
Uckfield,
East Sussex,
TN22 1RP.
0825 61611
Page 70

Broadway
See Horizon.
Pages 65, 66, 78, 80

Butlins Ltd,
Head Office,
Bognor Regis,
West Sussex,
PO21 1JJ.
0234 820202
Pages 24, 44, 46, 47, 48,
49, 50, 51

**Cabin Holidays,
Bull Plain,
Hertford,
SG14 1DY.
0992 59933
Page 40

**Camp Beaumont,
9 West St,
Godmanchester,
Huntingdon,
Cambs,
PE18 8HG.
0480 56123
Pages 122, 123

**Camping &
    Caravanning Club of
    Great Britain,
11 Lower Grosvenor
    Place,
London,
SW1W 0EY.
01-828 1012
Page 54

Camping for the Disabled,
20 Burton Close,
Dawley,
Telford,
Salop.
0743 68383
Page 130

**Canvas Holidays,
Bull Plain,
Hertford,
SG14 1DY.
0992 59933
Pages 87, 88, 90, 100

**Car Holidays Abroad
    Ltd,
Bull Plain,
Hertford,
SG14 1DY.
0992 54669

**Caravan Club,
East Grinstead House,
London Rd,
East Grinstead,
West Sussex,
RH19 1UA.
0342 26944
Page 54

Carousel Holidays Ltd,
PO Box 776,
Birmingham,
B4 712.
021-821 1366

Center Parks
See Sealink.

**Central Bureau for
    Educational Visits &
    Exchanges,
Seymour Mews House,
Seymour Mews,
London,
W1H 9PE.
01-486 5101
Page 119

**CHA
See Countrywide Holidays
    Association.

Channel Island Ferries,
Wharf Rd,
Portsmouth,
PO2 8RU.
0705 819416
Page 34

Character Cottages,
34 Fore St,
Sidmouth,
EX10 8AQ.
03955 77001
Page 41

CIE Tours,
Ireland House,
150/151 New Bond St,
London,
W1Y 9FE.
01-629 0564
Pages 40, 98, 107

Citalia,
Marco Polo House,
3-5 Lansdowne Rd,
Croydon,
CR9 1LL.
01-686 0677
Pages 23, 78

Civil Aviation Authority,
45-59 Kingsway,
London,
WC2B 6TE.
01-379 7311
Page 129

Club Cantabrica Holidays,
Holiday House,
146/148 London Rd,
St Albans,
Herts,
AL1 1PQ.
0727 33141
Pages 23, 64, 88, 89

Club Méditerranée,
106-108 Brompton Rd,
London,
SW3 1JJ.
01-581 4766
Pages 80, 81, 82, 85, 114

**Coastal Anti-Pollution
    League,
94 Greenway Lane,
Bath,
Avon,
BA2 4LN.
0225 317094
Page 13

Cosmos,
Cosmos House,
1 Bromley Common,
Bromley,
Kent,
BR2 9LX.
01-464 3488
Pages 23, 64, 65, 66, 75,
78, 80, 128

**Country Cottages in
  Scotland,
Claypit Lane,
Fakenham,
Norfolk,
NR21 8AS.
0328 4011
Pages 39, 41, 61

Countrywide Holidays
  Association,
Birch Heys,
Cromwell Range,
Manchester,
M14 6HU.
061-225 1000
Pages 61, 104

Crest Welcome Breaks,
Bridge St,
Banbury,
Oxon,
OX16 8RQ.
01-902 8877
Pages 22, 59, 60, 61

**Cricketer Holidays,
4 The White House,
Beacon Rd,
Crowborough,
East Sussex,
TN6 1AB.
08926 64242
Pages 22, 23, 78

**Cycling for Softies,
244 Deansgate,
Manchester,
M3 4BQ.
061-834 6800
Page 98

Danish Tourist Board,
169/173 Regent St,
London,
W1R 8PY.
01-734 2637
Page 68

DER Travel Service,
18 Conduit St,
London,
W1R 9TD.
01-486 4593
Pages 70, 108

DFDS Seaways,
199 Regent St,
London,
W1R 7WA.
01-434 1523
Pages 34, 150

**Disabled Drivers'
  Association,
Ashwellthorpe Hall,
Ashwellthorpe,
Norwich,
NR16 1EX
050841 449
Page 130

**Disabled Drivers'
  Motor Club,
1a Dudley Gardens,
London,
W13 9LU.
01-840 1515
Page 130

**Dolphin Adventure
  Holidays,
Grosvenor Hall,
Bolnore Rd,
Haywards Heath,
West Sussex,
RH16 4BX.
0444 458177
*Pages 110, 113, 122, 123,
124*

**EACH Cycling
  Holidays,
Tempo House,
15/17 Falcon Rd,
London,
SW11 2PJ.
01-223 6966
Pages 60, 97

**Early Learning,
Hawksworth Industrial
  Estate,
Swindon,
Wilts,
SN2 1TT.
0793 610171
Page 143

Ellerman Sunflight,
Travel House,
Broxbourne,
Herts,
EN10 7JD.
0992 87299
Pages 24, 65, 66, 80

**Enfants Cordiales,
13 Blackbrook Lane,
Bromley,
Kent,
BR2 8AU.
0322 76603
Pages 114, 116

**English Country
  Cottages,
Claypit Lane,
Fakenham,
Norfolk,
NR21 8AS.
0328 4041
Pages 39, 41, 61

**English Tourist Board,
Thames Tower,
Black's Rd,
London,
W6 9EL.
01-846 9000
Page 130

Enterprise Holidays,
British Airways Travel
  Shops/Travel Agents
  only.
Pages 23, 66, 78, 80

Enterprise Wintersports,
1 Wardour St,
London,
W1V 3HE.
01-439 7611
Page 116

**Eurocamp Travel,
1-6 Clay St,
Crawford St,
London,
W1H 3FS.
01-935 0628
Pages 87, 88, 89, 90

Falcon Holidays,
33 Notting Hill Gate,
London,
W11 3JQ.
01-727 0232
*Pages 23, 64, 66, 70, 74,
75, 77, 78, 80, 100, 102*

Family First,
See Lancaster Holidays.
Pages 64, 76, 77, 79, 80

**Field Studies Council,
Preston Montford,
Montford Bridge,
Shrewsbury,
SY4 1HW.
0473 850674
Page 96

Flair,
1 Wardour St,
London,
W1V 3HE.
01-734 4070

**Forest Holidays,
231 Corstorphine Rd,
Edinburgh,
EH12 7AT.
031-334 0066
Pages 39, 40, 54, 130

**Forestry Commission,
See Forest Holidays.

Fred Olsen Lines,
11 Conduit St,
London,
W1R 0LS.
01-409 3275
Pages 35, 70

French Leave,
21 Fleet St,
London,
EC4 1AA.
01-583 8383
Page 70

French Life,
456 The Strand,
London,
WC2R 0RG.
01-930 9583
Page 70

French Travel Service,
See Vacances Vertes.

French Villa Centre,
175 Selsdon Park Rd,
S. Croydon,
Surrey,
CR2 8JJ.
01-651 1231
Page 70

FreshFields (Europe),
PO Box 9,
Hayling Island,
Hants,
PO11 0NL.
0705 466111

**Gîtes de France,
French Tourist Office,
178 Piccadilly,
London,
W1V 0AL.
01-493 3480
Page 69

Global,
Glen House,
200 Tottenham Court Rd,
London,
W1A 2LS.
01-323 3266
*Pages 23, 64, 65, 66, 75,
80*

**Global Home Exchange
& Travel Service,
86 The Hall,
Foxes Dale,
Blackheath,
London,
SE3 9BG.
01-852 1439
Page 131

Go Greek,
See Sunmed.

Haven Holidays,
PO Box 20,
Truro,
Cornwall,
TR1 2UG.
0872 40000
Pages 48, 49

**Heinz Baby Club,
Vinces Rd,
Diss,
Norfolk,
IP22 3HH.
0379 51981

Hertz Rent a Car,
1272 London Rd,
London,
SW16 4XW.
01-679 1799
Page 144

Highlife Breaks,
PO Box 1 RA,
Newcastle upon Tyne
NE99 1RA.
091-232 1073

HF Holidays,
142/144 Great North Way,
London,
NW4 1EG.
01-203 6411
*Pages 61, 94, 96, 99, 100,
104, 105, 128*

**Holiday Care Service,
2 Old Bank Chambers,
Station Rd,
Horley,
Surrey,
RH6 9HW.
0293 774535
Page 130

Holiday Club
International,
See Horizon.
Pages 64, 67, 81, 83, 85

Holiday Fellowship,
See HF Holidays.

Holiday Inn Weekenders,
10/12 New College
Parade,
Finchley Rd,
London,
NW3 5EP.
01-586 8111
Page 59

APPENDIX 2. TRAVEL COMPANIES AND USEFUL ORGANISATIONS

Holimarine,
171 Ivy House Lane,
Bilston,
West Midlands,
WV14 9LD.
09073 77111
Page 48

**Home Interchange,
8 Hillside,
Farningham,
Kent,
DA4 0DD.
0322 864527
Page 131

Horizon,
Broadway,
Edgbaston Five Ways,
Birmingham,
B15 1BB.
021-632 6282
*Pages 63, 64, 65, 67, 75,
79, 80, 116*

Hoseasons Holidays,
Sunway House,
Lowestoft,
Suffolk,
NR32 3LT.
0502 87373
*Pages 40, 48, 55, 60, 70,
102*

Hoverspeed,
Maybrook House,
Queens Gardens,
Dover,
CT17 9BR.
01-554 7061
Pages 34, 70, 92

Inghams Travel,
329 Putney Bridge Road,
London,
SW15 2PL.
01-785 6555
Page 117

Inn-Tent Ltd,
See W H Smith Travel.
Pages 88, 90

Intasun,
Cromwell Avenue,
Bromley,
Kent,
BR2 9AQ.
01-290 0511
*Pages 23, 65, 67, 73, 75,
79, 80, 88, 90, 117*

**Interhome,
383 Richmond Rd,
Twickenham,
Middlesex.
01-891 1294
Pages 69, 71

**InterService Home
    Exchange,
Box 87,
Glen Echo,
Maryland,
20812,
USA.
Page 131

**Intervac,
6 Siddals Lane,
Allestree,
Derbyshire,
DE3 2DY.
0332 558931
Pages 130, 131

Irish Tourist Board,
150 New Bond St,
London,
W1Y 0AQ.
01-493 3201

Irish Youth Hostel
    Association,
39 Mountjoy Square,
Dublin 1.
0001-745 734
Page 105

Isle of Man Steam Packet,
Sea Terminal,
Heysham,
Lancs,
LA3 2XF.
0524 53046
Pages 34, 40

John Morgan Travel,
Meon House,
Petersfield,
Hampshire,
GU32 3JN.
0730 68621
Pages 111, 124

Just France,
Eternit House,
Felsham Rd,
London,
SW15 1SF.
01-785 9999
Page 70

Keycamp Holidays,
92-96 Lind Rd,
Sutton,
Surrey,
SM1 4PL.
01-661 1836
Pages 88, 89, 90

**Kiddy Mail,
Vinces Road,
Diss,
Norfolk,
IP22 3HH.
0379 4720
Pages 162, 163, 164

Ladbroke Holidays,
Only available through
    travel agents.
Pages 48, 49, 50, 51, 55

Ladbroke Hotels,
PO Box 137,
Watford,
Herts,
WD1 1DN.
0923 38877
Pages 45, 59, 60, 96

Lancaster Holidays,
29-31 Elmfield Road,
Bromley,
Kent,
BR1 1LT.
01-697 8181
*Pages 23, 64, 65, 67, 76,
79, 80, 128*

**Landmark Trust,
Shottesbrooke,
Maidenhead,
Berks,
SL6 3SW.
062882 5925
Page 39

Leisure Holidays,
25 Stephyns Chambers,
Bank Court,
Hemel Hempstead,
Herts,
HP1 1DA.
0442 51242
Page 48

Longship Holidays,
See DFDS.
Pages 70, 108

Magic of Italy,
47 Shepherds Bush Green,
London,
W12 8PS.
01-743 9555

**Mark Warner,
20 Kensington Church St,
London,
W8 4EP.
01-938 1851
Pages 81, 83, 85, 100

**Martin Rooks Holidays,
204 Ebury St,
London,
SW1 8UU.
01-730 0808
Page 79

Medallion,
642 Kings Rd,
London,
SW6 2DU.
01-731 2926
Page 79

Medina Holidays,
See W H Smith Travel.
Pages 79, 80

Meon Villa Holidays,
Meon House,
Petersfield,
Hants,
GU32 3JN.
0730 66561
Pages 63, 65, 70

**Millfield Village of
Education,
Street,
Somerset,
BA16 0YD.
0458 42291
Pages 95, 99

Modernline Holidays,
Hastings Rd,
St Helier,
Jersey.
0534 35511
Page 54

Mount Charlotte Hotels,
2 The Calls,
Leeds,
LS2 7JU.
0532 444866
Pages 45, 59

Mundi Color Holidays,
276 Vauxhall Bridge
Road,
London,
SW1V 1BE.
01-834 3492

Multitours,
21 Sussex St,
London,
SW1V 4RR.
01-821 7000
Pages 79, 80, 128

NAT Holidays,
Holiday House,
Domestic Rd,
Leeds,
LS12 6HR.
0532 450252
Pages 65, 80, 88

**National Association of
Holiday Centres,
10 Bolton St,
Piccadilly,
London,
W1Y 8AU.
01-499 8000
Page 49

National Holidays,
George House,
George St,
Wakefield,
West Yorks,
WF1 1LY.
0924 383838
Page 92

**National Trust,
36 Queen Anne's Gate,
London,
SW1H 9AS.
01-222 9251
Pages 39, 54

**NCT House Swap
Register,
69 Athelstan Rd,
Exeter,
Devon,
EX1 1SB.
0392 50310
Page 132

Neilson,
Holiday House,
Domestic Rd,
Leeds,
LS12 6HR.
0532 450252
Pages 117, 124

**Nelson's Mail Order,
5 Endeavour Way,
London,
SW19 9UH.
01-946 8527
Page 153

North Sea Ferries,
King George Dock,
Hedon Rd,
Hull,
HU9 5QA.
0482 795141
Page 34

**Northern Ireland
  Tourist Board,
River House,
48 High St,
Belfast,
BT1 2DS.
0232 246609

Norway Line,
Tyne Commission Quay,
Albert Edward Dock,
North Shields,
NE29 6EA.
0632-585555
Page 34

Olau-Line,
Sheerness,
Kent,
ME12 1SN.
0795 666666
Pages 35, 70, 150

Olsen Lines,
See Fred Olsen.

Olympic Holidays Ltd,
17 Old Court Place,
Kensington High St,
London,
W8 4PL.
01-727 8050
Pages 65, 67, 74, 79, 80

**One Parent Family
  Holidays,
See OPF Holidays.

**OPF Holidays,
25 Fore St,
Praze-an-Beeble,
Camborne,
Cornwall,
TR14 0JX.
020983 1274
Page 126

OSL,
Travel House,
Broxbourne,
Herts,
EN10 7JD.
0992 87299
Pages 24, 63, 65, 67

Paris Travel Service,
Bridge House,
Ware,
Herts,
SG1 9DF.
0920 3922
Page 92

Peter Stuyvesant Travel,
7 Percy St,
London,
W1P 9FB.
01-631 3278
Pages 83, 88

**PGL Young Adventure,
Station St,
Ross-on-Wye,
HR9 7AH.
0989 65556
*Pages 94, 95, 98, 100, 102,
  110, 122, 123, 124*

Phoenix Holidays,
Twyman House,
4th Floor,
16 Bonny St,
London,
NW1 9PG.
01-485 5515
Pages 79, 80, 84

**PleasureWood,
Somerset House,
Gordon Rd,
Lowestoft,
Suffolk,
NR32 1PZ.
0502 517271
Page 70

Pontin's Holidays,
Bridge St,
Banbury,
Oxon,
OX16 8RQ.
0202 295600
*Pages 22, 47, 48, 49, 50,
  51, 99, 128*

**Portland Holidays,
218 Great Portland St,
London,
W1N 5HG.
01-388 5111

**Preston Sunroutes Ltd,
4 Dollis Park,
London,
N3 1JU.
01-349 0311
Page 55

**Queensway Camping
  Hire,
Bells Ltd,
19-21 Queensway,
Bognor Regis,
West Sussex,
PO21 1QN.
0243 821769
Page 55

**RADAR,
25 Mortimer St,
London,
W1N 8AB.
01-637 5400
Page 129

**Rentatent,
Fifth Way,
Wembley Trading Estate,
Wembley,
Middlesex.
01-903 3473
Pages 52, 55

**Robertson
  Organisation,
44 Willoughby Rd,
London,
NW3 1RU.
01-435 4907
Page 119

**Royal Yachting
  Association,
Victoria Way,
Woking,
Surrey,
GU2 1EQ.
Page 100

Robinson Clubs,
See Olympic Holidays.
Pages 81, 84, 85

**RSPB Holiday Tours,
The Lodge,
Sandy,
Beds,
SG19 3DL.
0767 80551
Pages 60, 96

Sally Line,
54 Harbour Parade,
Ramsgate,
Kent,
CT11 8LN.
0843 595522
Pages 35, 69, 70

Scanhomes,
Scanscape Holidays,
68 Upper Thames St,
London,
EC4V 3BJ.
01-248 0431
Pages 70, 108

**Scottish Tourist Board,
23 Ravelston Terrace,
Edinburgh,
EH4 3EU.
031-332 2433
Page 55

**Scottish Youth Hostels
Association,
7 Glebe Crescent,
Stirling,
FK8 2JA.
0786 72821
Pages 44, 105

Sealink,
Travel Centre,
Victoria Station,
London,
SW1V 1JX.
01-834 8122
Pages 35, 40, 69, 70, 82, 92

**Seasons Holidays,
Edmundson House,
Tatton St,
Knutsford,
Cheshire,
WA16 6BG.
0565 3822
Page 89

**Single Parents Links
and Special Holidays,
See Splash.

**Ski Club of Great
Britain,
118 Eaton Square,
London,
SW1W 9AF.
01-245 1033
Pages 110, 124

Ski Enterprise,
See Enterprise
Wintersports.

**Ski Esprit,
1a Victoria Mews,
Victoria Rd,
Fleet,
Hants,
GU13 8DQ.
0252 616789
Pages 112, 113, 117

Ski MacG,
17 Old Court Place,
Kensington High St,
London,
W8 4PL.
01-351 5446
Page 124

Ski NAT,
See NAT Holidays.
Pages 113, 117

Ski Sunmed,
4-6 Manor Mount,
London,
SE23 3PZ.
01-699 5999
Page 117

Ski Val,
91 Wembley Park Drive,
Wembley,
Middlesex,
HA9 8HF.
01-903 4444
Pages 111, 124

**Ski West,
Eternit House,
Felsham Rd,
London,
SW15 1SF.
01-785 9999
Page 111

Ski Yugotours,
See Yugotours.

Skytours,
Greater London House,
Hampstead Rd,
London,
NW1 7SD.
01-387 9699
Pages 65, 79

**Small World,
Old Stone House,
Judges Terrace,
East Grinstead,
West Sussex,
RH1 1AQ.
0342 27272
Page 114

W H Smith Travel,
10 Regent St,
Swindon,
Wilts,
SN1 1JQ.
0793 31992
Page 24

SOL Holidays,
Churchfield House,
45-51 Woodhouse Rd,
London,
N12 9ET.
01-446 8500

**Splash,
Empire House,
Clarence St,
Swindon,
Wilts,
SN1 2JF.
0793 613220
Page 127

**Starvillas,
25/7 High St,
Chesterton,
Cambridge,
CB4 1ND.
0223 311990
Pages 67, 70, 128

**Summer Cottages,
Dorchester,
Dorset,
DT1 1RE.
0305 67545
Pages 39, 41

**Summer University,
Centre for Extension
   Studies (BR),
University of Technology,
Loughborough,
Leics,
LE11 3TU.
· 0509 267494
Page 96

Sunair,
351 Oxford St,
London,
W1R 1FA.
01-629 1123
Pages 79, 80

Sunmed Holidays,
4-6 Manor Mount,
London,
SE23 3PZ.
01-699 7666
*Pages 21, 63, 64, 65, 67,
   80, 100, 128*

**Sunsites,
Sunsites House,
Dorking,
Surrey,
RH4 1YZ.
0306 887733
Pages 87, 88, 89, 90

Suntours,
Madeira House,
Corn St,
Witney,
Oxon,
OX8 7BW.
0993 76969
Pages 79, 80

**Sunvista Holidays,
5A George St,
Warminster,
Wilts,
BA12 8QA.
0985 217373
Page 70

**SuperTed Holidays,
Llandrindod Wells,
Powys,
LD1 5LE.
0597 2600
Page 60

Supertravel,
22 Hans Place,
London,
SW1X 0EP.
01-589 5161
Pages 111, 112, 113, 124

Susie Madron's Cycling
   for Softies,
See Cycling for Softies.

Swiss Travel Service,
Bridge House,
Ware,
Herts,
SG12 9DE.
0920 61221
Page 17

TAG Adventure Holidays,
Rhydybont,
Talgarth,
Powys,
LD3 0EE.
0874 711346
Page 99

Tapeworm,
32 Kingsway,
London,
SW14 7HS.
01-878 9532
Page 143

Tentrek,
152 Maidstone Rd,
Sidcup,
Kent,
DA14 5HS.
01-302 6426
Page 89

THF Breaks,
24-30 New St,
Aylesbury,
Bucks,
HP20 2NW.
01-567 3444
Pages 45, 59, 60

Thomas Cook Holidays,
PO Box 36,
Thorpe Wood,
Peterborough,
PE3 6SB.
0733 502234
*Pages 24, 63, 65, 67, 80,
   117*

**Thomas Cook Medical
Centre,
45 Berkeley St,
London,
W1A 1BD.
01-499 4000
Page 152

Thomson Holidays,
Greater London House,
Hampstead Rd,
London,
NW1 7SD.
01-387 9321
*Pages 22, 63, 64, 67, 73, 74,
   76, 79, 80, 92, 117, 128*

Time Off,
Chester Close,
Chester St,
London,
SW1X 7BQ.
01-235 8070
Page 92

Timsway Holidays,
Penn Place,
Rickmansworth,
Herts,
WD3 1RE.
0923 771266
Pages 63, 80, 128

**Tjaereborg,
7/8 Conduit Street,
London,
W1R 9TG.
01-499 8676
Pages 65, 74, 76, 128

Tourauto,
Bridge House,
Ware,
Herts,
SG12 9DG.
0920 3050
Page 70

Touropa Britain,
52 Grosvenor Gardens,
London,
SW1W 0NP.
01-730 8860
Pages 20, 69

Townsend Thoresen
    Ferries,
Russell St,
Dover,
Kent,
CT16 1QB.
0304 203388
Pages 35, 70, 92

**Travel Club of
    Upminster,
54 Station Rd,
Upminster,
Essex,
RM14 2TT.
04022 25000
Pages 23, 63, 67

**Triskell Cycle Tours,
28 New King St,
Bath,
BA1 2BL.
0225 312832
Page 98

Trust House Forte Hotels,
See THF Breaks.

TUI,
See Touropa Britain.
Page 69

**Vacances,
28 Gold St,
Saffron Walden,
Essex,
CB10 1EJ.
0799 25101
Page 70

**Vacances
    Franco-Britanniques,
1 St Margaret's Terrace,
Cheltenham,
Glos,
GL50 4DT.
0242 526338
Page 70, 71

Vacances Vertes,
Francis House,
Francis St,
London,
SW1P 1DE.
01-828 8131
Page 70

Villa Seekers,
See French Life.

VFB,
See Vacances
    Franco-Britanniques.

Wales Tourist Board,
Bridge St,
Cardiff,
CF1 2EE.
0222 27281
Page 99

Warner Holidays,
94 Baker St,
London,
W1M 2HD.
01-379 7938
Pages 47, 48, 49, 50, 51

Welsh Country Cottages,
Claypit Lane,
Fakenham,
Norfolk,
NR21 8AS.
0328 51341
Page 39

Wings Holidays,
Travel House,
Broxbourne,
Herts,
EN10 7JD.
0992 87299
Pages 74, 79, 80

Worldwide Home
    Exchange Club,
45 Hans Place,
London,
SW1X 0J2.
01-589 6055
Page 132

YHA Travel,
14 Southampton St,
London,
WC2E 7HY.
01-240 5236
Page 95

Youth Hostels
    Association,
Trevelyan House,
8 St Stephens Hill,
St Albans,
Herts,
AL1 2DY.
0727 55215
Pages 89, 105

Youth Hostel Association
    of Northern Ireland,
56 Bradbury Place,
Belfast,
BT7 1RU.
0232 224733
Page 105

Yugotours,
150 Regent St,
London,
W1R 6BB.
01-439 7233
Pages 79, 80, 117, 129

Index

If you are looking for tour operators or other organisations, refer to the list on pages 169–179. Numbers printed in **bold** type indicate main entry.

Notes